"Informative, interesting, and full of useful real-life examples. I could not help imagining myself as an orchestra conductor, directing the 'rhythm' of my business."

—**Mark Skaletsky**, President and CEO,
GelTex Pharmaceuticals, Inc.

"There has been no handbook before *The Rhythm of Business* that has provided such a concrete definition of the entrepreneurial process."

—**Shayne F. Gilbert**, President/CEO and Founder,
Silverweave Interactive

"For those people who may not feel they are natural entrepreneurs, *The Rhythm of Business* will provide them with a process that captures the very essence of what it takes to be successful in business, both today and tomorrow."

—**Buddy Carp**, President, New World Technologies, Inc.

"*The Rhythm of Business* swings!"

—**John A. Seeger**, Professor of Business, Bentley College

THE RHYTHM
OF BUSINESS

THE RHYTHM
OF BUSINESS

The Key to Building and Running Successful Companies

JEFFREY C. SHUMAN

WITH DAVID ROTTENBERG

Butterworth-Heinemann

Boston Oxford Johannesburg Melbourne New Delhi Singapore

Butterworth–Heinemann supports the efforts of American Forests
and the Global ReLeaf program in its campaign for the betterment of
trees, forests, and our environment.

Cover design by Stephanie Pierce-Conway

Library of Congress Cataloging-in-Publication Data
Shuman, Jeffrey C., 1945–
    The rhythm of business : the key to building and running
successful companies / Jeffrey C. Shuman with David Rottenberg.
        p.   cm.
    Includes bibliographical references.
    ISBN 0-7506-9991-4 (alk. paper)
    1. Success in business.   2. Entrepreneurship.   I. Rottenberg,
David, 1946– . II. Title.
    HF5386.S4467   1998
    650.1—dc21   97-35195
                                                              CIP

British Library Cataloguing-in-Publication Data
A catalogue record for this book is available from the British Library.

The publisher offers special discounts on bulk orders of this book.

For information, please contact:

Manager of Special Sales
Butterworth–Heinemann
225 Wildwood Avenue
Woburn, MA 01801-2041
Tel: (781) 904-2500
Fax: (781) 904-2620

For information on all Butterworth–Heinemann books available, contact our
World Wide Web home page at: http://www.bh.com

10 9 8 7 6 5 4 3 2 1

Printed in the United States of America

To my entrepreneurial wife, Penny, and
our daughters, Rachel and Alison,
for their love, understanding,
and unfailing belief in me.

Janet Axelrod, employee number one at the Lotus Development Corporation, says that the process of creating the company was "understanding how to do a dance, really that's all it is. You start moving your hips this way and your shoulders the other way. Fit yourself into the music, and make it work just right." Mastering this dance is about giving up the attachment to permanence, to certainty, to being in control, to playing from the sheet music. When you've mastered the dance, you no longer need to follow the markings of the foot chart on the floor.

…JOHN KAO, *JAMMING: THE ART AND DISCIPLINE OF BUSINESS CREATIVITY*, 1996, P. 161

Contents

About the Authors

Jeffrey C. Shuman has crafted a unique career as an entrepreneur, consultant, business professor, and author. He is considered a leading expert in the emerging field of entrepreneurial studies and has founded or been part of the founding team of four businesses. He has served as a consultant to dozens of entrepreneurs, and his courses in entrepreneurship tap state-of-the-art knowledge about business creation. His writings include dozens of articles and a book on entrepreneurs and the business creation process.

Jeff received his doctorate in management from Rensselaer Polytechnic Institute. Since then, he has pursued a dual career as an entrepreneur and business educator. Jeff's businesses have included two giftware manufacturing and stationery distributors, a microcomputer software publishing and marketing company, and a microcomputer hardware manufacturer and distributor. In 1983, Jeff joined the faculty of Bentley College, where he now is a full professor, teaching entrepreneurship, and is the founding director of Bentley's Entrepreneurial Studies Program. Currently, Jeff is on the Advisory Board of Streamline, Inc., a consumer services startup company.

David Rottenberg heads his own marketing and computer documentation company. He also works as a free-lance author and has written business profiles for *Boston Magazine* and computer-related articles for several national computer publications. Other work includes writing and producing informational videos on business and computer topics.

There is no limit to the good one can do if he or she doesn't care who gets the credit.

...PROVERB

Acknowledgments

Early in my life, my parents, Bertha and Max Shuman, and most of my older relatives owned their own businesses. I remember growing up thinking that owning your own business was something everyone did. Obviously, this is not the case, but my earliest thoughts about business were related to the excitement and challenges our families experienced running these small businesses.

Years later, when I became involved in several startup businesses myself, I benefited greatly from having had the opportunity to work with and learn from Gerald Eber, Pushi Dhingra, Lew Ginsburg, Al Shapiro, Bob and Becky Ronstadt, Michael Shane, and Tim DeMello.

While at Babson, Jack Hornaday and David Rogers were instrumental in helping me develop a much better conceptual understanding of business. At Bentley, Tony Buono and John Seeger have played important roles, listening to me for endless hours as I talked through the underpinnings of *The Rhythm of Business*. I also want to thank Rudy Winston and Andrew Zacharakis for their willingness to "field test" early versions of the manuscript in their entrepreneurship courses at Bentley.

A special thanks to Barry Abrams, Stephen Berman, Buddy Carp, Steve DeBenedictis, David Fialkow, Pat Flynn, Judy George, Shayne Gilbert, Alan Hoffman, Jim Howell, David Litos, Dennis O'Conner, Ruth Owades, Faith Popcorn, Mark Skaletsky, and Joe Weiss for reading early drafts of the manuscript and providing helpful suggestions. Thanks also to Jane Forte, Virginia Karamanian, and Terry Tierney for helping prepare and reproduce all the drafts of the manuscript.

During the past two years, as *The Rhythm of Business* was transformed from my thoughts to paper, David Rottenberg, my friend and collaborator, helped turn my words into a coherent manuscript and helped shape many of the ideas in this book.

A heartfelt thanks to Stephanie Pierce-Conway. Without her graphic design creativity, I would never have visualized the dance so clearly.

Over the past nine months, the fortunes of *The Rhythm of Business* have improved immeasurably because of the support and encouragement of my agent, Doris S. Michaels, and her assistant, Dahlia Porter. When the pressures of getting the book published became intense, Doris's dedication to the project always got me through.

At Butterworth-Heinemann, I would like to thank Karen Speerstra and Stephanie Gelman Aronson, whose valued editorial input helped the book reach its final form.

Years ago, Dame Edith Sitwell noted that "Rhythm is one of the principal translators between dream and reality." Clearly, the contributions of my teachers, friends, business associates and family has enabled my dream to become reality.

Jeffrey C. Shuman
Framingham, Massachusetts
April 1997

Do not follow where the path may lead.
Go instead where there is no path
and leave a trail.

…UNKNOWN

Introduction

The conventional wisdom is wrong! As surprising as it may seem, the standard advice on how to start, build, and run a business more often leads to failure than success. What's taught in business schools, written in business books, and passed on as gospel from one businessperson to another is not the methodology that successful businesspeople follow. The conventional wisdom states that to start, build, and run a business you have to identify and evaluate an opportunity, develop a business concept, assess and acquire resources, manage the venture, and then harvest and distribute value.[1] And the conventional wisdom also holds that a successful businessperson possesses certain characteristics, including commitment, perseverance, a tolerance for risk, and a high level of integrity and reliability.[2]

Even though there are variations on this advice and reams of instructions on how to master each element, the basic belief is that you begin with an idea, and if the idea is good and you transform that idea into reality, you end up with a successful business. If the idea is bad or you stumble in transforming it into

[1]Howard H. Stevenson, Michael J. Roberts, and H. Irving Grousbeck, *New Business Ventures and the Entrepreneur* (Boston: Irwin, 1994), pp. 17–33.
[2]Jeffry A. Timmons, *The Entrepreneurial Mind* (Andover, MA: Brick House Publishing Company, 1989), pp. 30–49.

reality, your business fails and you end up with a loss and, perhaps, bankruptcy. However, this "wisdom" simply isn't true.

In his landmark book, *Innovation and Entrepreneurship*,[3] famed management guru Peter Drucker observed:

> When a new venture does succeed, more often than not it is in a market other than the one it was originally intended to serve, with products or services not quite those with which it had set out, bought in large part by customers it did not even think of when started, and used for a host of purposes besides the ones for which the products were first designed.

And Leo Kahn, the retailing entrepreneur who founded Purity Supreme Supermarkets and cofounded Staples (a national chain of office-supply superstores), noted:[4]

> The entrepreneur has to grow with the concept. If you look at any business that is started and successful five years later it is very different in many ways from the original concept. And the entrepreneur has got to know when to change and when to be rigid in sticking to the original principle.

Peter Drucker and Leo Kahn both make a very profound and very important point: **Most businessmen and -women do not succeed by bringing into reality the idea with which they begin**. Why? Because every business goes through a natural development process. This development process is so natural and so intimate a part of business life that it has been overlooked and misunderstood even by those individuals who guide their businesses through the process.

So many times we hear successful businessmen and -women talk about their success as if it were a mystery. But it is not a mystery. It is a rhythm—*the rhythm of business*—and it lies hidden in the cacophony of everyday events, and even when it

---

[3]New York: Harper and Row, 1985, p. 189.
[4]Steve Bailey and Steven Syre, "Retailer Leo Kahn Gets Back to Nature," *The Boston Globe* (August 21, 1996), p. F2.

is heard, it is heard only dimly and followed mostly by instinct. Entrepreneurs who are successful might know the conventional wisdom—they've read the same books, gone to the same schools, and listened to the same experts as everyone else—but when it comes to what really makes them succeed, they follow their "gut" and therefore can't describe their technique for success. And, if those who've been there and done it can't explain it, who can? Certainly not the academic observers and theoreticians who only observe business from the outside. As a result, the very essence of business has remained unexplained; and for those involved in the world of business, there has always lurked a terrible sense of fear, a sense of being slightly lost, of being slightly out of sync because no one completely understands where they are or what they are doing or where they are heading within the overall context of gaining and maintaining business success.

Writing in *Inc.* magazine, Barry Diller, the former chairman of Paramount Pictures and now chairman and CEO of Silver King Communications, succinctly sums up the irony and paradox that has long surrounded business success:[5]

> What all my [business] experiences have had in common is a battle, a holy war if you will, between process and expertise. . . . Process is fundamentally a human function. . . . And process can't be forced or rushed. It works for everyone, not just the four or five real geniuses out there. For them, God bless them, instinct is enough. For the rest of us there's process. What is this process? If I could put it clearly, I would.

Even though Diller has experienced success, even though he lives it in his own life, all he can say about it is that he knows it is a process. What that process is—how it works, how anyone can follow it—he feels but can't explain.

And, unfortunately, no one else can, either. Until now!

---

[5]Barry Diller, "The Discomfort Zone," *Inc.* (November 1995), p. 20.

The development process that Diller and other successful businesspeople "feel but can't explain" is what I call the rhythm of business. From my own experience living business on the inside, my academic background, and years of working closely with successful entrepreneurs observing business on the outside, I have uncovered and described the development process that intuitively all natural-born businesspeople use when starting, building, and running a successful business.

The Rhythm of Business is not just another theory or philosophy. At its very heart, the rhythm of business is business: it is how all businesses develop and it is the beat to which all business flows. Business ideas and business concepts are not static but respond to the lead of the market. Business is not a store or a product or a spreadsheet, it is a dance. And the beautiful thing about realizing this is that merely understanding and following the simple precepts described in *The Rhythm of Business* will change forever how you think about and manage a business. The failures and successes no longer will be failures and successes but part of a learning cycle. The business concept used to launch a business, product, or service no longer will be cast in stone but a stage in the ongoing development that every business goes through. The information you gather will not be mere data but keys to unfolding future market opportunities. The love you feel for a business will not be something to hide or think of as simply pride but one of the major keys to business success.

A lot of business books deal in "tips." They tell you how to close a sale or how to climb the corporate ladder or how to win every negotiation. This book does not do that. This book deals with the most fundamental principles of business.

Fundamental principles might sound uninteresting to someone who is trained to think in terms of the practicalities of daily business life, but in fact, **The Rhythm of Business is the most practical, down-to-earth business book you will ever read**. Let me remind you of what Peter Drucker said:[6]

---

[6] Drucker, p. 189.

When a new venture does succeed, more often than not it is in a
market other than the one it was originally intended to serve,
with products or services not quite those with which it had set
out, bought in large part by customers it did not even think of
when started, and used for a host of purposes besides the ones
for which the products were first designed.

Two practical examples of this phenomenon are the businesses of Ray Kroc and Henry and Richard Bloch. Kroc started
in business selling ice-cream milk shake mixers and ended up as
the multibillionaire owner of McDonald's. The Bloch brothers
started out as ordinary accountants and ended up founding H &
R Block, the national income tax preparation chain. How does
the conventional wisdom explain this transformation? The conventional wisdom says it occurred by "instinct," "luck," "determination," "drive," "being in the right place at the right time,"
and the like, which is to say the conventional wisdom doesn't
explain it at all.

In reality, the success of Ray Kroc and Henry and Richard
Bloch is due to the plain fact that they followed the rhythm of
business. And the equally plain fact is that you, too, can follow
the rhythm of business. Of course, I don't mean that reading this
book will magically turn you into a millionaire but it **does** mean
that if you read this book you will understand what the rhythm
of business is and follow the rhythm of your own business better than you ever have before and thus stand a better chance of
business success.

The importance of *The Rhythm of Business* cannot be over-
emphasized. Many people understand important parts of this
process: they know that you have to love your business, they
know that you have to satisfy your customers, they know that
you have to have information. But, they don't understand that
these elements are not isolated "tips" but part of an overall process, a process that until now has never been identified and
explained.

What is new in this book is not the specific elements that
make up the rhythm of business. What is new is that there is a

rhythm and that all the elements of business fall into the specific pattern that make up this **rhythm**.

Instinctively, natural-born businesspeople always have followed this rhythm and most often followed it to success. Other business people, without this instinctive rhythm, have had only the conventional wisdom and too often followed it to failure.

As with many insights, the difference between the conventional wisdom and the rhythm of business is merely a different way of looking at many familiar elements. But, once this new insight is grasped, once this new beat is heard, it will make a great difference between how you start, build, and run your business.

Today, with only the conventional wisdom as a guide, business people typically expect that they will "identify and evaluate an opportunity, develop a business concept, assess and acquire resources, manage the venture, and then harvest and distribute value." The problem arises when, inevitably, natural market forces require the business to grow, not according to the artificial dictates of written business plans, but according to organic market realities. In this dynamic situation the conventional wisdom breaks down, the business flounders, and those responsible become lost and confused and think they have somehow or somewhere failed and all too often actually do fail.

But once you understand the rhythm of business, you will never feel lost or out of sync, no matter what business you are in or what stage of development your business has reached. You will always know where you are, what you are doing, and where your business is heading because *The Rhythm of Business* incorporates a process with concrete steps to attain business success applicable for any individual, whether in a large corporation or a new business.

Some people have an intuitive ability to feel the rhythm of business. Others have to work at developing that ability. But everyone has rhythm. It's inborn, to some degree, in all of us. And, just as you can learn to feel the rhythm of dance and song, you can learn to feel the rhythm of business and you can learn to be successful in the business world.

Part I

The Rhythm of Business

If you can walk
You can dance
If you can talk
You can sing
...A SAYING FROM ZIMBABWE

1

Rhythm

Flash! *InfoWorld* says, "Bill Gates has rhythm!"[1] And *InfoWorld* is right. Bill Gates definitely has rhythm.

But the kind of rhythm I'm talking about is not the usual kind of rhythm. It's not the rhythm of a Stevie Wonder, an Aretha Franklin, a Fred Astaire, or a Ginger Rogers. The kind of rhythm I'm talking about is *the rhythm of business;* and if anyone has rhythm, it's Bill Gates. How do I know? Because Bill Gates tops *Forbes'* list of the ten richest people in the world.[2]

What does rhythm have to do with business? And is rhythm really the key to success? The *American Heritage Dictionary* defines *rhythm* as, "The regular patterned flow, the ebb and rise, of sounds and movement in speech, music, writing, dance, and other physical activities, and in natural phenomena."

[1]Robert X. Cringely, "Notes from the Field," *InfoWorld* (January 15, 1990), p. 94.
[2]"The Superrich," *Forbes* (July 15, 1996), p. 125.

So, we can say that *rhythm* refers to "patterns," patterns that we can not only see or hear but feel, taste, or smell, as well. These patterns, these rhythms are very important in human life.

> Rhythm is undeniably the structuring basis of life on this planet ... The sun's rays create the primary rhythms of rest and activity, of growth and decay, of life and death ... Realizing that healthy living things are not only internally rhythmic but are also synchronized with their environment, the earliest communities of humans based their survival on keeping track of these rhythms.[3]

Whether in art, song, dance, literature, sports, love, or recreation, all human activity follows a rhythm. And, not surprisingly, this rhythm also runs through business. Rhythm is basic to how business functions.

Let's look again at Bill Gates. In the late 1980s, Gates's company, Microsoft, spent millions of dollars developing a software product called Windows. When it was first introduced it failed. Reviewers hated it. Consumers didn't buy it. Rival software execs gloated that Gates was losing his touch. But Bill Gates wasn't deterred. He learned from his failure. He spent several million more dollars and a few years later came out with a second version of Windows. It was better, but still not good enough. It also failed. Bill Gates tried again. A few years more and many millions of dollars later, Microsoft introduced its third version of Windows, and suddenly it was an "overnight" success. Microsoft revolutionized the PC business and made billions of dollars.

Does all this mean that stubbornness and persistence pay off? Not really. Stubbornness and persistence can just as easily and many times more often mean failure and bankruptcy. What this example does mean is that there is a **rhythm** to business, a pattern that all businesses follow, no matter what product or service they sell; a rhythm that we all can understand and learn from to help us build and run a successful business.

---

[3]Layne Redmond, "When the Drummers Were Women," *Earth Star* (August–September 1994), p. 11.

WHAT IS THE RHYTHM?

Most simply, the rhythm of business is attempting to develop a product or service that fulfills a group of customers' wants and needs, testing the product or service in the marketplace, learning from that test, and then refining the product or service to more accurately fulfill your customers' wants and needs. Every successful business, to a greater or lesser degree, follows this rhythm. Those businesspeople who have a "natural rhythm" follow it well; those who don't, follow it less well. But no matter how good or bad your "natural" rhythm is, once you understand what the rhythm is and how important it is, you will follow it better and improve your ability to feel the rhythm of business.

To be successful in business you have to have rhythm. Bill Gates has it. Consciously or unconsciously, he followed this rhythm when he developed Windows. Bill Gates knew that his customers wanted and needed a simpler, more graphical computer operating system, so Microsoft developed Windows. After it was developed, naturally, the firm tested it in the marketplace. It wasn't right, so the company brought back the product and worked on it. After another test it still wasn't right. So, the company did some more work, tested it some more, and this time, helped by improvements in the speed of computer hardware, Windows was a sensation and Bill Gates had done it again. But, what had Bill Gates really done? Very simply, he had followed the rhythm of business; developing, testing, and refining a product or service until it was right.

Oftentimes, when we read in books or articles about some very successful businessperson, the author seems unable to identify and describe what accounts for the subject's success. Writers use words like she had that "ineffable something—call it instinct, or even genius." But the truth is, that "ineffable something" is not mystical or magical. It's not some sixth sense. That "ineffable something" is the rhythm of business.

Consider how Ron Shaich, cofounder of Au Bon Pain, Inc. (sales of $259 million through 231 company-owned and 58 franchised bakery cafes), describes his recipe for success: "The way you build a business is you continue to dance."[4] In other words, he always is developing his company's ability to fulfill his customers' wants and needs. When Ron talks about dancing, he's not using this description as a metaphor. He's saying that he really has rhythm—that he's continually researching, developing, analyzing, and refining his business by coming up with new products and business concepts, testing them in the marketplace, and devising new ways to make them better. Ron never stops dancing to the rhythm of business.

ARE SUCCESSFUL BUSINESSPEOPLE BORN OR MADE?

Whether successful businessmen and -women are born or made always has been a controversy. Obviously, this is an important issue. If successful businesspeople are born, then it could be assumed that, at some point, their inborn intuition somehow will awaken and lead them down the path to business success. Conversely, those without that special intuition shouldn't try to start and run a business. But, if successful businesspeople are made, then perhaps anyone interested in becoming successful can do so after finding out what the ingredients are.

Actually, I believe that successful businesspeople are both born and made. But, there is a difference between the two types just as there is a difference between someone we would describe as having "natural, inborn" athletic skills and someone who practices a lot and plays hard.

Take basketball, for example. It's not surprising that, when Larry Bird, a natural-born athlete, was asked to what he attributed his success, he answered, "I always knew where the ball was going to be." And, when Wayne Gretzky, another natural-born athlete, was asked essentially the same question, he replied, "I skate to where the puck is going to be." How do they know where the puck or the ball is going to be? They know because they feel

[4]Chris Reidy, "Cooking up a Recipe for Success Through Refining Product Mix," *The Boston Globe* (May 17, 1994), p. 56.

the inborn rhythm of the game, which allows them to process information in such a way that, instinctively, they sense what they need to do and where they need to be at any given point in time.

But, what about all the other thousands of basketball and hockey players around the world, professional and amateur, do all of them have the inborn rhythm of a Wayne Gretzky or a Larry Bird? Obviously, the answer is no. That doesn't mean that those individuals can't work hard and become much better or even great. Everyone in the NHL and the NBA isn't a Wayne Gretzky or a Larry Bird. The NBA and NHL have all different levels of players just as there are all different levels of business-people. Not everyone is a Bill Gates or a Ron Shaich but that doesn't mean you can't be successful.

DEVELOPING THE RHYTHM OF BUSINESS

We can say that there are six basic requirements to developing the rhythm of business:

1. You need, at least, some natural skills.
2. You need to work hard and practice.
3. You need a basic understanding of the mechanics of the business you are in.
4. You need to gather information about your business.
5. You need to constantly think about your business.
6. You need to love your business with a passion.

Interestingly, of the six, the least important is having some natural-born skills, because, whether or not you have any natural, inborn ability, if you work hard, if you understand the basic mechanics of your business, if you gather information about your business (such as talking to your customers and reading trade magazines and books like this), if you constantly think about your business, and if you love your business, you have all the ingredients to improve your natural rhythm and become successful. For example, **one of the most important points I will make in this**

**book is that a key component of the rhythm of business is fail-
ure.** It took Bill Gates three tries before he succeeded with Windows. In fact, Microsoft has a history of not getting its software
products right the first time. As Eric Schmidt in *US News & World
Report* has commented, "Microsoft's role and power in the industry are stunning. No other company could routinely release such
weak first versions of its products, then use its own customers as
a test group for revisions until it gets a fully working product."[5]
But Microsoft's first releases are not "failures." Rather they are the
first steps in the rhythm of business. In a recent television interview, Gates had this to say about listening to his customers:[6] "We
appreciate the feedback we get from customers. Every time they
calls us, we write that down and we use that to make a better
product." And, in the same interview, he added:

> It is true that if you find an idea that requires three or four years
> of improvement and patience and really sticking with it, that
> we're very good at that. Take Windows, which we bet the com-
> pany on. Everybody doubted that would succeed—IBM did not
> support us in that. It took longer than we expected, over four
> years, before finally, graphical interfaces got popular and now
> people take it for granted. It's part of every personal computer
> and you just expect it to be there. That was one of the grand suc-
> cesses of the company.

But Gates's success is not just vision, or persistence, or ideas,
or market clout. It's a specific pattern. When Gates begins developing a product, he allows for "failure" in his business plan.
Intellectually or instinctively, he dances to the rhythm of business
and makes the correct decision that he will continue to develop
his product, bring it to market, listen to his customers' wants and
needs, and refine his product until it becomes a success.

---

[5]Eric Schmidt, "The Struggle For Bill Gates's Soul," *U.S. News & World Report*
(November 25, 1996), p. 71.
[6]Transcript from "The Road Ahead," *The Charlie Rose Show* (November 25,
1996).

This is the rhythm of business. It's a rhythm that anyone can understand and follow and into which all the down-to-earth aspects of business, such as financing, researching, negotiating, manufacturing, marketing, advertising, and managing, fit. You have to know how to plan for failure as well as success because both are part of the rhythm of business.

No one can devise a perfect business plan. It doesn't matter how good your business instincts are. It doesn't matter how hard you work. It doesn't matter how much you understand business or how much you love it. Too many variables are involved and the variables change too quickly for any one person or group of people to ever start and run a perfect business. **This means that change is inevitable in business and anything that changes follows a rhythm.**

THE FIRST BEAT

Where does the rhythm of business begin? It begins with the first beat. To start a successful business, first you need to have an idea about a product or service that fulfills a potential group of customers' wants and needs. Once you have that idea, you need to learn as much as you can about the exact nature of your customers' wants and needs. Then, you have to design a business that best fulfills those wants and needs—you have to decide how to make the product, how to market the product and how to distribute the product, and so forth. Then, of course, you have to actually open for business. But, as mentioned, no matter how well you've planned, no matter how good your instincts are, no matter how hard you've worked, no matter how much you understand your business, and no matter how much you love your business, change is inevitable, because the only way you can truly understand your customers is from direct contact with them.

All the analysis of secondhand market research is good only for a start. True understanding of your customers' wants and needs begins when you open for business—whether it's your first day or the thousandth. At that point, you have to be ready to analyze your customers' responses and refine your business according to their actual wants and needs. You have to be ready to come up with new ideas—new ads, new methods of distribution, new manufacturing technologies, new features, new pricing, and so on—to make your business more accurately fulfill your customers' desires. The faster you learn how to develop, test, analyze, and refine, the faster your business grows and the more profitable it becomes.

For example, let's say you're starting a business and you think there's a market opportunity selling theater tickets in malls. First, you do as much research as you can to see whether the idea has merit. Maybe your research simply consists of you and your spouse walking through malls asking shoppers questions. Maybe you hire a professional research firm. No matter what type and level of research you use, the results have to be good enough to convince not only you but potential investors to put their hard-earned cash into bringing your idea to reality. You need to know what type of malls work best, what type of tickets you should sell, how much of a surcharge your customers are willing to pay, how many sales people are required at each booth, and the like. When you feel you have a viable business plan and enough money to start, you open for business.

You want to adjust your business according to your customers' responses as quickly as possible, so it's good to start small. Let's say you start with one booth in one upscale mall, selling tickets primarily to theater events. However, much to your surprise, you discover that your largest response is from teenagers buying tickets to rock concerts. So, after analyzing those results, you hire younger help, redesign your booth with posters of rock stars, and open up in a couple of more malls heavily frequented by teenagers. Then, of course, the cycle begins again. You receive more customer responses, analyze those results, make more changes, and go back into the marketplace. As you can see, each cycle brings you closer and closer to that ever-alluring but idealized point where your business perfectly fulfills your customers' wants and needs.

This natural development process never stops. Even after you've been in business for years, profitably selling tickets in dozens of malls, you must never stop the process. You must never stop the dance!

Having the rhythm of business means that you understand and feel the timing for this entire process—developing, testing, analyzing, and refining your business based on continual customer input. If you have an inborn business rhythm, it takes fewer cycles before your product or service is successful. If your business rhythm is less good, it takes more cycles. But, once you understand what the rhythm is, whether you are a born businessperson or a made businessperson, you can improve your business rhythm and be successful.

To return to the sports metaphor, not every athlete plays in the "big leagues" or earns a gold medal or wins at Wimbledon. In the same way, not every successful businessperson breaks into the *Forbes* list of the ten wealthiest. The reality is that, just as at any point in time there are only a few thousand professional athletes, at any point in time there are only a few thousand $100 million entrepreneurs. But whatever the level of your game is, it's important to take every step you can to develop your potential and make your business as successful as possible.

I started this chapter with a saying from Zimbabwe:

If you can walk
You can dance
If you can talk
You can sing

And that's the real point. Everyone has rhythm. It's inborn to some degree in all of us. And just as you can learn to feel the rhythm of dance and song, you can learn to feel the rhythm of business, and you can learn to be successful in the business world.

This book is about the rhythm of business and what you can do to improve your rhythm. Chapters 1 through 4 focus on understanding and feeling the rhythm of business. Chapters 5 through 9 describe the practical steps you can use to start, grow, and run a business by following the natural rhythm of business. Chapter 10 completes our journey and starts yours. It's important to learn how to dance but it's even more important to start dancing.

KEY POINTS IN CHAPTER 1

• The standard advice on how to start, build, and run a business is wrong. The conventional wisdom states that you have to identify and evaluate an opportunity, develop a business concept, assess and acquire resources, manage the venture, and then harvest and distribute value.

• But that advice is incorrect. Most businessmen and -women do not succeed with the idea with which they begin because every business goes through a natural development process, which I call *the rhythm of business*.

• The rhythm of business is attempting to develop a product or service that fulfills a group of customers' wants and needs, testing the product or service in the marketplace, learning from that test, and then refining the product or service to more accurately fulfill your customers' wants and needs.

• There are six basic requirements to developing the rhythm of business:

1. You need, at least, some natural skills.
2. You need to work hard and practice.
3. You need a basic understanding of the mechanics of the business you are in.
4. You need to gather information about your business.
5. You need to constantly think about your business.
6. You need to love your business with a passion.

• You have to know how to plan for failure as well as success, because both are part of the rhythm of business.

• Just as you can learn to feel the rhythm of dance and song, you can learn to feel the rhythm of business, and you can learn to be successful in the business world.

As I watched the seagulls, I thought:
That's the road to take; find the absolute
rhythm and follow it with absolute trust.

...NIKOS KAZANTZAKIS

2

Understanding the Rhythm

Being in business evokes a lot of different feelings: the satisfaction of pleasing customers, the potential for making lots of money, and the excitement of being your own boss; yet at the same time, there's the fear and uncertainty about whether your company will survive and prosper in the ever-changing business world. Fortunately, you're not alone. You don't have to fly solo or fly by the seat of your pants. A lot of help is available from people, from books, and from courses. Each makes its points, which you have to evaluate and adapt. **In this book, the most important point is that business is not a store or a factory or an office. Business is a rhythm. And it is basically the same rhythm whatever type or size of business you are in.**

While you may be familiar with some of the steps in the rhythm, or even all of the steps, it is critical that you understand that they are not separate and unrelated but part of a whole and that you need to make this whole an ingrained part of your thinking. You must develop an instinctive understanding of what needs to be done, when it needs to be done, and why it needs to be done, if you are going to be successful in business.

In Chapter 1, we said that to start and run a successful business you need to learn as much as possible about your customers' wants and needs. You also must determine which business concept is best able to provide your customers exactly what they want and need. We also emphasized that this process is ongoing. You must continue to dance. Even after a business is started, you must continually refine it based on actual customer input and then relaunch its products or services so that the business always comes closer and closer to satisfying customers' real wants and needs. This repetitive cycle is how business progresses, and having the rhythm of business means that you "feel" the timing for and understand the nature of each step in this cycle.

CUSTOMERS CREATE THE RHYTHM

To build and run a successful business, a customer orientation is needed. Customers drive business and create its basic rhythm. You have to satisfy their wants and needs, not the other way around. Customers care little about your wants and needs. The risks associated with business decrease with increasing knowledge of your customers. Far too many businesspeople talk a lot about the marketplace without ever getting into the nitty gritty of customers: who they are and what they really want and need.

GETTING IDEAS FOR BUSINESSES

When we look at the history of successful businesses, we find that, particularly for a new entrepreneur, the best place to start and run a company is in an area already known, perhaps from past work experience or a hobby. For example, if your interest is in computers, you have a better idea of other computer users' wants and needs than airplane pilots' wants and needs. And that knowledge means you'll be better able to identify an opportunity, better able to develop a business or a new product or service to satisfy that opportunity, and better able to understand your customers' responses to your efforts so that you can continue to refine your business. You'll also have a better understanding of future technological developments to keep abreast of customer demand and changing business strategies.

Of course, if you believe that you have identified a business opportunity in an area where you have no prior experience or knowledge, it does not mean that you cannot or should not pursue that opportunity. What it does mean is that it will take you longer and cost you more to develop the required understanding of who your customers are and what kind of business will satisfy their desires better than any other business in the world.

What if you see a significant opportunity in a new industry or in an industry undergoing radical transformation, perhaps due to technological innovation? In a radically changed or new industry, you most likely have little relevant preexisting knowledge. But there is a major difference between seeing an opportunity in a new industry versus seeing an opportunity in an existing industry about which you have no prior knowledge. In the new industry, most likely all potential competitors are starting with the same limitation; whereas, if the opportunity is in an existing industry, one or more competitors also may see the same opportunity and have preexisting knowledge that may enable them to satisfy your customers before you do.

CHANGING AS YOUR CUSTOMERS CHANGE

However, even after you've found your market opportunity, opened your business, and begun satisfying your customers' wants and needs, you still must never lose sight of your customers. Why? Because your customers' wants and needs are not static. They change over time due to a wide variety of factors, such as politics, technology, lifestyles, and economics. The dynamic nature of your customers' wants and needs naturally complicates the task of trying to satisfy them. It means you are trying to zero in on a moving target. The longer it takes to zero in, the more likely your customers' wants and needs will have changed. It is true that customers' wants and needs change faster in some industries than in others. But, no matter how fast or slow they change, the point is they do change. And, as they change, your product or service and your business methods also must change.

Far too many companies go out of business or struggle to stay alive because their CEOs fail to keep pace with changes in the wants and needs of their customers. It's as if, having once gone through the task of successfully identifying a viable product or service and a profitable method of marketing it, they become obsessed with keeping that original business concept intact, long after it has lost its ability to satisfy customers.

Entrepreneurs who have had one success often think they can ride that success forever. They can't. Success never is final. At any moment, a product or service or business concept may no longer satisfy customers, and you have to be both alert to that and ready to change. An Wang is a perfect example of a businessman who, in the fast-moving computer industry, failed to change. Wang had a great product, a dedicated word processor, but when personal computers appeared that could run a variety of software applications, Wang refused to change and stuck with his more expensive and limited product. In a few short years, his company went from a multibillion-dollar success to a multibillion-dollar bankruptcy. Why? Because An Wang refused to see the necessity of changing his product to satisfy his customers' changing wants and needs. Unfortunately, it's an example that we see all too often.

And, it happens not just in the fast-paced technology-based industries. Look at the athletic footwear industry. For years companies like Converse and Keds were the market leaders. Yet, out of nowhere, companies like Nike and Reebok catapulted to the top because they understood that consumers were becoming more interested in jogging, aerobics, and other sports that demanded footwear specifically designed for those activities. Converse and Keds lost sight of their customers and didn't see their changing wants and needs and thus lost their leadership. And it happened because they didn't understand the rhythm of business. They didn't understand that a successful business is not a done deal but a process, and change is basic to the process. Your objective is to go to the marketplace with the product or service and the business concept best able to satisfy customers today as well as tomorrow. If you don't keep pace with your customers, your competitors will.

Let's take another look at Nike and Reebok. Now that they are at the top of the athletic footwear industry, they can't stop keeping track of their customers. The sneaker business has gone from a stodgy industry to a fashion conscious industry and new trends such as sports utility footwear are always appearing. So, if Reebok and Nike don't want to follow in Converse and Keds's footsteps, they need to continue to refine their products and continue to satisfy their customers or some new company, like a Timberland or a Skechers, will.

DIAGRAMMING THE DANCE

For those who like explanations with charts and graphs, take a look at Figure 2–1. In this simple diagram, I've represented the *Level of Understanding of Your Customers' Wants and Needs* along the vertical axis and *Time and Cost* along the horizontal axis.

As you can see, I've also positioned two points on the figure and labeled them *Starting Level of Customer Understanding* and *Profitable Level of Customer Understanding*. The *Starting Level of Customer Understanding* represents how much you know about your customers' wants and needs at the time you first identify a marketplace opportunity (whether it's a new business or a new approach for an existing business). How far up the vertical axis the starting level is positioned is based on how good your initial understanding of your customers' wants and needs is.

Again, the greater your preexisting knowledge of your customers, the greater your initial understanding of your customers' wants and needs and the closer you'll be to the point I have labeled the *Profitable Level of Customer Understanding*, where to some degree you have satisfied your customers' wants and

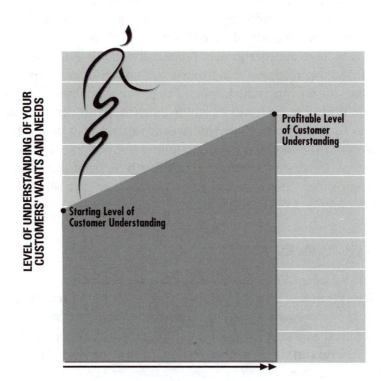

Marketplace Opportunity
Figure 2–1

needs and the business has started to make a profit. To build a successful business, you must move to **at least** the level of understanding of your customers' wants and needs represented as profitable. However, acquiring this increased understanding and insight takes time and costs money. In Figure 2–1, the time and cost are shown as the horizontal line.

The amount of time and money is influenced by many factors, such as how well acquainted you are with your customers and how much research you do. However, for the moment, keep in mind that, as always **in business, the main objective is to get to the profitable level of customer understanding as quickly and as inexpensively as possible**.

An oft repeated statistic is that "approximately 80 percent of new businesses fail within the first five years." This high failure rate in large part is due to a business running out of time and money before it reaches a profitable level of understanding. And, remember what makes reaching this profitable level more difficult and expensive is that your customers' wants and needs change.

In addition to understanding your customers' wants and needs, you have to identify the business concept that best satisfies these wants and needs. Clearly, if you do not understand your customers, you can't identify the best business concept. For example, if your customers are interested primarily in a product at the lowest cost, your business might work best delivering the product through mail order or a warehouse store; whereas if your customers require knowledgeable sales help or are interested in snob appeal, a fancy store front in a fashionable part of town with good parking might be necessary. All too often, businesses fail when an opportunity is correctly identified but the business concept used doesn't satisfy the customers' **actual** wants and needs. However, once you understand the rhythm of business, what you can see is that the real cause of the failure is not that the business goes to the marketplace with the wrong concept. No one person (or team) is able to take into account all of the factors required for success. Mistakes in business are inevitable. The real cause of the failure is that the company isn't flexible enough or prepared enough to change. Business is an ongoing process. You must get into the rhythm of business and follow it so that your ability to satisfy your customers continues to increase.

However, I should note here that it's a lot easier to change an idea than a business, so whenever you are planning, be as creative and flexible as possible. Consider every alternative. In a book I wrote a few years ago with Bob Ronstadt, we expressed the view that numerous ways exist to build and run a business and the first idea is rarely the best.[1] Seek out as much information as you can and identify as many business concepts as possible, no matter how wild they may seem. Don't limit yourself. Do not evaluate or critique them until you've identified all possibilities.

Do you want the firm to be a research company or a company that focuses on the production of products or one concerned mainly with distribution? Perhaps, your established business is in the midst of changing from a production company to a distribution company, or your venture encompasses two or all three of these activities. Whenever you are in the planning step, each new business idea should be considered carefully, following the implications as far out into the future as you can. Some ideas will be practical; some ideas will be impractical. For instance, the skills needed for a company marketing directly to consumers are considerably different from the skills needed to sell to retailers. And each business concept has a very different impact on the amount of money and other resources you need. It doesn't matter at this point that your thinking is speculative. It has to be speculative because you're in the idea phase of your business.

Let's look at another chart for a moment. Figure 2–2 helps visualize the task of how to build the best business concept. I

[1]For a more complete discussion of how to generate alternative venture concepts please refer to Robert Ronstadt and Jeffrey Shuman, *Venture Feasibility Planning Guide: Your First Step Before Writing a Business Plan* (Natick, MA: Lord Publishing, 1988).

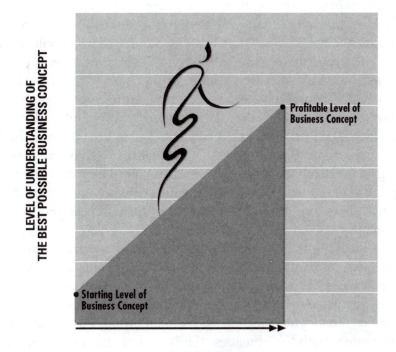

Business Concept

Figure 2–2

again use the vertical axis to represent *Level of Understanding* and the horizontal axis to represent *Time and Cost*. This time, the vertical axis represents your *Level of Understanding of the Best Possible Business Concept*.

As in Figure 2–1, two different points are shown on the diagram: *Starting Level of Business Concept* and *Profitable Level of Business Concept*. When you first think about your business, you're not really sure what business concept you should use, but you probably have a few ideas, so the starting level is positioned near but not at the bottom of the *Level of Understanding* axis. Once you receive actual feedback from your customers, your level of understanding will grow until you're able to identify a profitable business concept. As before, the horizontal line represents the *Time and Cost*. Again, speed is extremely important because the longer it takes to get to a profitable business concept, the higher the cost and the greater the chance that you will run out of money or a competitor will beat you to the punch.

Speaking of competition, it's important to realize that, in business, competition is not the same as it is, for instance, in tennis. In tennis, to win, you have to beat your opponent. In business, you have to beat your opponent but, more important, you have to satisfy your customers. Too many times businesspeople are content with their business if it is "better" than their competition. For example, if the best of the competition ships a customer's order in seven days and you somehow figure out a way to ship in three days, you may feel that you're sure to get the customer's order. However, if your customers need one day shipping, even though you're the fastest in the industry, you still are not satisfying your customers. Instead, you're leaving an opportunity for a new competitor who will put both you and your current competitors out of business.

A classic example of this mistake is what happened to American automobile manufacturers in the 1970s and 1980s. All Ford was interested in was building a better car than General Motors and Chrysler. And General Motors and Chrysler were interested only in building a better car than Ford. Not one of the three was interested in satisfying their customers' actual wants and needs, which left a gaping hole in the market for inexpensive, high-quality, energy-efficient Japanese cars. No matter how much American automobile manufacturers might have complained about market dumping, outdated factories, high salaries, and the like, at the heart of their failure was taking their eyes off their customer. As soon as Detroit started building cars that Americans wanted, Americans bought them.

The key to building and maintaining a successful business is not about being "better" than the competition. It is about satisfying customers. If your focus is just on bettering the competition, you in fact may wind up beating the competition but still losing. However, if you stay focused on satisfying customers, you are sure to beat your competitors.

Of course, I'm not saying that you shouldn't identify your competition, analyze what it does well, and try to do better. You need to do that in the process of building and running a business. But if your main focus is on being better than the competition, you are focusing on the wrong thing. **Satisfying your customers is the only way to achieve lasting success and realize the full profit potential of your business.**

THE NEVER-NEVER LAND OF THE IDEAL BUSINESS

Figure 2–3, a combination of Figures 2–1 and 2–2, illustrates the goal of business—perfectly satisfying your customers' wants and needs using the best possible business concept. As before, the vertical axis represents the *Level of Understanding* but this time it refers to both *Your Customers' Wants and Needs* and the *Best Possible Business Concept*. The horizontal axis again represents *Time and Cost*.

Notice how the chart shows that, when you first identify a marketplace opportunity, you need to learn as much as you can about the **true nature** of your customers' wants and needs and that, as your understanding of your customers grows, your

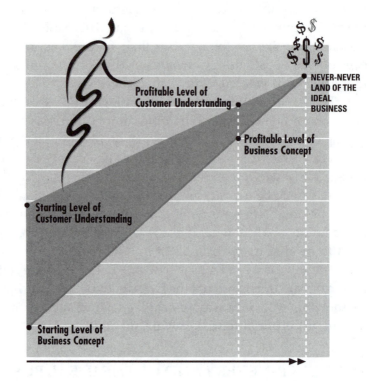

TIME AND COST

Your Vision
Figure 2–3

understanding of the best possible business concept grows. The goal is reached at the point represented in Figure 2–3 as the ideal business: where you have complete understanding of your customers' wants and needs and the business concept best able to fill them.

In reality, of course, no one ever reaches that ideal point, but the chart serves as a prod to remind you that, when planning, you should have a vision of what your business would look like if you could reach that point. For example, when Bill Gates started Microsoft, he expressed his vision of his company as "A computer on every desk and in every home, all running Microsoft software."[2] Even though your vision is your goal, it always must be subject to change. Today, Microsoft is heavily involved in news, CD-ROMs, and the Internet, which probably were not part of Bill Gates's original vision of his company. But that has not mattered to Gates's success and it will not matter to yours. As your business experience deepens and your business gets closer and closer to understanding its customers, your vision will come into sharper focus. But it's by having a vision and moving toward it that you start the process that is the rhythm of business.

And remember, the point on the chart that represents the ideal business is not fixed. It's a moving target because customers' wants and needs change over time, and business methods change. Like the legendary Maltese falcon, it is a treasure you always chase but never reach. After all, Bill Gates has one of the world's most successful companies but, if he wants to stay at the top of the fast-paced world of personal computers, he still has to keep dancing. As he readily acknowledges, "We're in a business where no amount of success guarantees future success."[3] But, in business, that is where the excitement and the opportunities lie. The constant change of customers' wants and needs and the constant introduction of new business methods and new technologies creates the openings for both old and new companies to grow.

[2]James Gleick, "Making Microsoft Safe for Capitalism," *The New York Times Magazine* (November 5, 1995), p. 53.
[3]Amy Cortese, "The Software Revolution," *Business Week* (December 4, 1995), p. 81.

DOING THE DANCE—STEP BY STEP

How do you take advantage of these openings in the marketplace? Through the rhythm of business—coming up with ideas for products or services that satisfy customers' wants and needs, continually testing the ideas in the marketplace, analyzing the results of the tests, and then refining your business based on the results of your analysis. **Repeatedly going through these steps throughout the life of a company—in other words, continuing to dance—is how your understanding of your customers and the "best" business concept grows.** This ongoing cycle is the rhythm of business, and it is a rhythm every businessperson has to follow if his or her business is to gain and maintain success. The more aware you are of the cycle and the more accurately you follow it, the better your business grows. Below, I define the four distinct steps that make up what I call one *customer interaction cycle* in the ongoing rhythm of business. And remember, this cycle is true whether your business is old or new, large or small, employs thousands or just one—you.

Step 1. Planning is identifying a product or service based on an understanding of customers' wants and needs; selecting a flexible, low-cost business concept to deliver those products or services; and determining the resources needed to carry out your plans.

Step 2. Preparation is doing everything necessary to "prepare" your products or services so that they are ready for sale when you open for business. Preparation also includes establishing the business concept selected in step 1. More than any other step of the cycle, step 2 entails making hundreds of detailed decisions and taking hundreds of detailed actions as you gain access to and deploy the resources needed for step 3.

Step 3. Interaction involves bringing your product or service and business concept to the marketplace by opening your doors for business and interacting with your customers. No matter how long you've been in business, every time you interact with your customers you should consider that you are "testing" your product or service.

Step 4. Analysis and refinement is evaluating the results of the interaction and refining your understanding of your customers' wants and needs and of your business concept based on the results of your analysis of the customer interaction carried out in step 3.

Figure 2–4 illustrates how the steps in the rhythm of business develop your understanding of your customers' wants and needs and of the best possible business concept from your starting levels of understanding to where your business approaches the ideal level. The positioning of step 1 (Figure 2–5 is a detailed close-up of one complete customer interaction cycle) reflects that you have begun the business development process. Step 2 is where you prepare to move into your customers' "space" and "interact" with your customers. Step 3 is when you actually interact with your customers (i.e., you are open for business), and step 4 is when you analyze the information gathered in step 3 and refine your understanding of your customers and your business concept. As you can see from Figures 2–4 and 2–5, every customer interaction cycle follows a rhythm—the rhythm of business—going back and forth as you try out new ideas, test the ideas, analyze the results of the tests, and then develop a better product or service and a better business concept to more fully satisfy your customers. And as you can see from Figure 2–4, this cycle repeats and repeats as you move closer and closer to the ideal business. It never stops!

GETTING IN TUNE

In the Introduction to this book I stressed a very important observation from Peter Drucker:[4]

> When a new venture does succeed, more often than not it is in a market other than the one it was originally intended to serve,

---

[4]Drucker, 1985, p. 189.

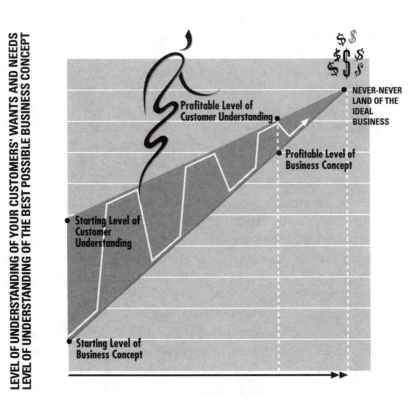

The Rhythm of Business:
A Series of Customer Interaction Cycles
Figure 2–4

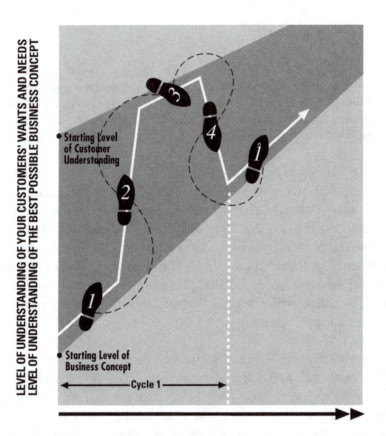

Customer Interaction Cycle Close-up
Figure 2–5

with products or services not quite those with which it had set out, bought in large part by customers it did not even think of when started, and used for a host of purposes besides the ones for which the products were first designed.

And from Leo Kahn:[5]

The entrepreneur has to grow with the concept. If you look at any business that is started and successful five years later it is very different in many ways from the original concept. And the entrepreneur has got to know when to change and when to be rigid in sticking to the original principle.

With the steps of the rhythm of business in mind, we can now understand very clearly the truth of Peter Drucker and Leo Kahn's observations. **The reason successful businesspeople end up in businesses that they didn't plan is because successful businesses aren't planned. They grow, which doesn't mean that planning doesn't take place. Planning is step 1 of every customer interaction cycle. But planning also is followed by steps 2, 3, and 4, which means change, and the primary reason for change is your customer.**

Like Columbus, a businessperson sees an opportunity and bravely starts out to fulfill that opportunity. Along the way, reality gets in the way. For Columbus, reality was discovering America rather than a new route to India. For every businessperson, there probably are many realities but **the ultimate reality is the customer**. And the rhythm of business not only anticipates the intrusion of this ultimate reality but gives you a method of how to deal with each new reality, big or small, as it comes along.

When you look at the steps in the rhythm of business, you can see that they always bring you more in tune with the customer, because by following the rhythm of business, you change from what **you** think is the ideal business to what the

[5] Bailey and Syre, 1996, p. F2.

customer wants as the ideal business. And, of course, for this transformation to take place, your ideas and your business must change. Change is part of the process. Change is part of the rhythm of business. Thus, the four steps involved in the rhythm of business not only verify Drucker and Kahn's astute observations but explain how and why the changes take place.

For example, look at what happened to Rebecca Matthias's business:[6]

Rebecca Matthias started Mothers Work in 1982 to sell maternity clothing to professional women by mail order. Mail-order businesses are easy to start, but with tens of thousands of catalogs vying for consumers' attention, low response rates usually lead to low profitability—a reality Matthias confronted after three years in business. In 1985, she borrowed $150,000 to open the first retail store specializing in maternity clothes for working women. By 1994, Mothers Work was operating 175 stores generating about $59 million in revenues.

Or how about Doug Chu and Scott Samet's business:[7]

To get started selling healthier movie snacks to theater chains, Chu and Samet bought little packages of dried fruit, yogurt pretzels and the like from convenience stores. Strapped for cash, they decided to personally deliver their wares to local theaters, and send packages via UPS to those farther afield. In July 1992 Chu and Samet quit their Bankers Trust jobs, capitalized their new venture with $15,000 of saved Bankers Trust bonus money and placed some orders for snacks.

One of Chu's first sales calls was to a childhood friend, Bruce Corwin, president of a Los Angeles-based 100-screen theater chain. Corwin agreed to test (Chu and Samet's) Taste of Nature's snacks in two Santa Barbara theaters. No go.

Corwin's concession manager explained that the packaging turned customers off. Not appetizing like the sight and smell of fresh popcorn. Why not differentiate their snacks by taking them

[6]Amar Bhide, "The Questions Every Entrepreneur Must Answer," *Harvard Business Review* (November–December 1996), p. 125.
[7]Marla Matzer, "Healthy Choice," *Forbes* (September 25, 1995), p. 176.

out of their packages and displaying them in bulk? Chu and Samet installed clear plastic bins from which concession workers scooped out Taste of Nature's products. That got sales moving . . .

Another example is Thomas L. Massie, who was flying through the $5.4 million raised in an initial stock offering in 1993 for his third company, Focus Enhancements Inc.:[8]

> "I was getting the crap kicked out of me by the vendors, the ana-lysts were beside themselves, the stock was trading at an all-time low," recalls Massie, 34. "My wife and I were drinking a cup of tea, talking about it, and I'm saying, 'This is the hardest thing I've ever done in my life.'"
>
> That's when Massie had "a strong revelation," said Steve Loewengart, a stock analyst for H.J. Meyers & Co. in New York. "He was about to lose his company."
>
> But today, the troubled company is off the mat and on the comeback trail. Woburn [Massachusetts]-based Focus Enhance-ments eked out a profit of $107,000 in the first half of this year [1995]. While hardly a fortune, it's a marked improvement over combined losses of $10 million in 1992 through 1994.
>
> The company's flirtation with profits is a product of its trans-formation from a mail-order house for Macintosh computer periph-erals to a producer of computer networking components and multimedia display systems based on Focus-owned technologies.
>
> No longer sold by catalog, Focus products line the shelves of computer superstores. Under contract with Apple Computers, Focus is developing combination graphics and networking cards for the newest line of PowerBook Laptops.

These stories are typical of most businesses, and as you can see, the skill of the businesspeople involved lies not so much in following their original business plans as in eventually getting an understanding of what their customers wanted. Yet, even that was done in a stumbling way. And just this stumbling shows us the errors of the conventional wisdom. Under its spell, most people write their business plan and stick to it. And when

[8]Robert Keough, "Shift in Focus Enhances Survival Odds," *The Boston Globe* (October 15, 1995), p. 43.

their business is built, if they discover that their business does not satisfy their customers, they think they've failed, or that their ideas are no good, or that they lack some other important characteristic of business success. And if they've spent all their money on this one "go," then they quickly go out of business, which is why I am emphasizing that **business is not a specific business. It is a process. It is a rhythm, and if you follow the rhythm, you will plan for change and not spend all your capital thinking you can get it right the first time.**

GETTING "IT" RIGHT—EVENTUALLY

In business, no one gets it right the first time. You have to listen to your customers, listen to your employees, listen to your vendors, listen to your investors, and eventually, by following the rhythm of business, you will succeed as Drucker and Kahn noted—most likely in a different market than the one you started with different products and services sold to different customers but, most important, with a profit that allows you to continue to change and grow as the wants and needs of your customers change and grow.

I've gone on here because the points are so important, but I would like to return to our charts for just a moment before I end this chapter. When you look at the diagrams of the rhythm of business, keep in mind they are just that—diagrams. Depending on the business you are in, this whole process—steps 1–4—may not be done in neatly marked cycles but simultaneously. For example, each time you want to analyze the results of interacting with your customers, you may not be able to completely stop doing business. Some businesses, such as mail-order catalogues and 1-900 information provider services, lend themselves to clearly delineated cycles; other businesses, such as restaurants and retail stores, may require interacting and refining simultaneously.

The difference is like that between football and soccer. In football, the offense has the ability to huddle after each play. The team has the opportunity to assess what has happened during the last play and decide what to do next. It can change players. It even can change the entire game plan. Soccer is different. The team lacks the ability to stop playing the game and huddle. It has to do the assessment and make the changes on the run. The practical realities of business more often are like soccer than football, and complicating the rhythm even further, the lines between the steps are blurred. In every step, you have to deal with some planning, you have to deal with some details, you have to deal with some analysis. Also, different parts of your business may be engaged in different steps of a customer interaction cycle at the same time. For instance, in the theater ticket business, you may be interacting with your customers in one mall while planning to open booths in three other malls. But these complexities and varieties again are what makes business exciting and challenging and are why I emphasize that business has rhythm.

FEEL THE TIMING

In every customer interaction cycle, you must keep a watchful eye on how much time is elapsing and how much money you are spending. When you "feel" the time is right, you move your business on to the next step. And in saying "when you **feel** the time is right," I mean that the endpoint of each step in a customer interaction cycle often is hazy. For example, with the theater ticket business, while you might have a goal of opening your first booth in the Fall, the preparation which takes place during step 2 may not be finished by the Fall, which means you either have to open not completely ready or delay your opening. In this situation and others like it, how do you know when it's right to move onto the next step? You have to "feel" when it's right. It might be when you're 50 percent ready or 70 or 90 percent. When you do begin step 3—open your first booth in a mall—how much time do you need to judge your customers' response? In Chapter 1, I said theater tickets sold poorly but rock tickets sold well; but that is a very general statement. As the decision maker, when do you have enough information to say definitively that theater tickets sold poorly? Maybe that Fall there were few good shows but many good rock concerts. Maybe a large employer in the area had a big layoff. Maybe your advertising wasn't targeted to the right audience or in the correct newspapers. Any business decision always encompasses a million maybes, which is why, in the end, after you've considered all the "hard" data, your decisions always come down to a "feeling."

So, your timing, which is the moment you put your "feelings" into action, is very important and yet very difficult to determine. Unfortunately, there are no set rules. No one is standing on the sidelines signaling to you. Yet "feeling" that point in time—when the benefits to be gained from continuing in one step or moving onto the next—is essential. Knowing that there is a rhythm and the steps in the rhythm is the "knowledge" aspect of the rhythm of business. Timing is the intuitive aspect of the rhythm of business and in Chapters 3, 4, 8, and 10, we talk about how to increase your ability to "feel" the timing for moving between the different steps of any one customer interaction cycle. However, for now, what should be clear is that completing a cycle in the rhythm of business leads to an increase in your level of understanding of your customers' wants and needs and an improvement in your business concept's ability to satisfy these wants and needs. Each time you finish a cycle, you should see an increase in customer sales. Of course, during any cycle, it is possible to misread your customer feedback or get insufficient feedback and temporarily go in the wrong direction. But, if you understand the rhythm of business and run a business with it in mind, you will be able to correct your mistakes in the next cycle.

NEVER STOP DANCING

In all the excitement over improving sales, make sure that you do not stop the process. You can **never** develop the perfect business. The most anyone can hope to achieve is a near perfect business for a specific point in time. Next week, next month, next year, next decade, what you are doing today may be completely wrong. So, don't lose the rhythm. You must continue to dance. You must continue leading your business through the steps of one customer interaction cycle after another. Once you stop dancing, the business loses its ability to change, and any business that cannot change is in jeopardy of falling prey to the latest trends, the newest technologies, or a new competitor.

Take another look at Figure 2–4. You can see, in our example, that it took three customer interaction cycles to reach a profitable business concept. However, another individual having identified the same marketplace opportunity could create an entirely different business concept and take a different number of cycles. But, no matter what business is created and no matter how many cycles it requires, **the process is the same**. There is a rhythm to business and the most critical element in this rhythm is your ability to "feel" when the time is right to move between each step of any one customer interaction cycle. As you develop your ability to feel when it is time to move between these steps, you will be developing your ability to feel the rhythm of business.

As I said, if you have an inborn rhythm, it takes fewer repetitions of the cycle for your product or service to be successful. If your business rhythm is less good, it takes more repetitions. But, once you understand the process and use it, your rhythm will improve **and** your business will improve. And once you have found the rhythm of business, you need to follow it with absolute trust. The more you do, the better your business will be.

KEY POINTS IN CHAPTER 2

• Business is not a store or a factory or an office; business is a rhythm. And it is basically the same rhythm whatever type or size of business you are in.

• Because customers drive business and create its basic rhythm, you need to learn as much as possible about your customers. You also must determine which business concept is best able to provide your customers exactly what they want and need.

• The best place to look to start and run a company is in an area already known, perhaps from past work experience or a hobby.

• The main objective is to get to the profitable level of customer understanding as quickly and as inexpensively as possible.

• The key to building and maintaining a successful business is not about being "better" than the competition; it is about satisfying your customers.

• The four steps of every customer interaction cycle are

 Step 1. Planning is identifying a product or service based on an understanding of customers' wants and needs; selecting a flexible, low-cost business concept to deliver those products or services; and determining the resources needed to carry out your plans.

Step 2. Preparation is doing everything that has to be done to "prepare" your products or services so that they are ready for sale when you open for business. Preparation also includes establishing the business concept selected in step 1. More than any other step of the cycle, step 2 entails making hundreds of detailed decisions and taking hundreds of detailed actions as you gain access to and deploy the resources needed for step 3.

Step 3. Interaction involves bringing your product or service and business concept to the marketplace by opening for business and interacting with your customers. No matter how long you've been in business, every time you interact with your customers you should consider that you are "testing" your product or service.

Step 4. Analysis and refinement is evaluating the results of the interaction and refining your understanding of your customers' wants and needs and of your business concept based on the results of your analysis of the customer interaction carried out in step 3.

• Repeatedly going through the steps of the rhythm of business (planning, preparation, interaction, analysis, and refinement) throughout the life of a company—in other words, continuing to dance—is how the growth of your understanding of your customers and the growth of your understanding of the "best" business concept takes place.

• A natural-born businessperson understands he or she is not starting a business but a process, and the process is the rhythm of business.

• In business, no one gets it right the first time nor is success ever final.

• Completing a cycle in the rhythm of business leads to an increase in your level of understanding of your customers' wants and needs and an improvement in your business concept's ability to satisfy those wants and needs.

• The endpoint of each step in a customer interaction cycle often is blurred.

• The most critical element in this rhythm is your ability to "feel" when the time is right to move between the steps of a customer interaction cycle.

• Knowing that there is a rhythm and the steps in that rhythm is the "knowledge" aspect of the rhythm of business; timing is the intuitive aspect of the rhythm of business.

As a general rule the most successful man in life is the one who has the best information.

...BENJAMIN DISRAELI

3

Information: Learning to Read the Score

My appreciation for the role information plays in the rhythm of business comes in large part from Michael B. Shane. During 1990 and 1991, I worked closely with Michael as part of the founding team of Model American Computer Corporation. Before Model American, Michael had started, built, and sold five multimillion-dollar businesses and had been called a visionary entrepreneur by *The Wall Street Journal*, *Business Week*, and *Time* magazine. It was a fascinating experience for me, because Michael Shane is not only someone who has a natural, inborn business rhythm but he also has a profound intellectual understanding of the workings of business. In particular, he is such a strong advocate of the importance of information that much of what I discuss in this chapter is based on what I absorbed from Michael during those two very intense years.

The word *information*, although centuries old, has become so widespread that it is almost impossible to pick up a newspaper or magazine or turn on a television or radio without finding numerous references to it. We used to hear that the three keys to success in business were location, location, location. Today, we know the answer is information, information, information. Almost every day multibillion-dollar companies are making multibillion-dollar deals to better position themselves for the revolution taking place along the electronic information super-highway.

The problem, however, is that, with all the attention information gets, after a while you tune it out. You stop listening when you hear someone talking about information. And that's unfortunate. Because if you are going to feel the rhythm of business, you must understand the importance of information and realize that it isn't so much a word or a revolution as a technique.

WHAT IS INFORMATION?

According to Michael Shane, in its most general sense, information is anything,[1] anything that can be discerned with your senses and your intellect. It is every idea, theory, conjecture, experience, or philosophy, and it can be found anywhere—in books, magazines, TV, computers, movies, people. The value of information, in Michael's favorite phrase, comes when you "gather, process, and connect it." That's something we all do instinctively every day, but rarely do we examine exactly how it's done. For example, if we want to open an ice-cream parlor and sell the best homemade ice-cream, one of the first things we do is gather all the information we can about making ice-cream. Next, we process the information, which means thinking about it, analyzing it, putting it in a comprehensible form. And then we connect it. We see what it's telling us. In this example, that means seeing the patterns in the information and coming up with new recipes or, if this were a different example, perhaps, a new marketing technique or a new distribution channel.

---

[1] For a complete discussion of Michael's views on information, see his book, *How to Think Like an Entrepreneur* (New York: Bret Publishing Limited Partnership, 1994).

SEEING THE PATTERNS

Seeing the patterns in information is a lot like the game of connect the dots we played as kids. Take a look at Figure 3–1. What do you see? If you're not sure, go ahead and connect the dots. I started you off by connecting a few dots. Think of every dot as a bit of information. When you start, the paper is full of separate dots. As long as the bits of information remain separate, the design on the paper is meaningless. As you connect the dots, as you process the information, the design on the paper becomes clearer until, finally, you have enough lines to see the pattern, to have an understanding, to get an idea.

Sometimes, you can figure out the pattern with only a few lines. Sometimes, you need more lines. Sometimes, you need all the lines. But eventually the light dawns.

Remember, the person who wins the game is the person who sees the pattern first. It's just the same in business. The businessperson who wins the game is the one who sees the patterns first and incorporates them into his or her business. It may be in creating a new product or a new, inexpensive way of manufacturing or discovering a new customer group. But the point I want to make is that most people pick up information by accident and do not actively engage themselves in analyzing the information once they pick it up. However, when in business, you can't rely on accidents or be lazy in your thinking. You have to make gathering, processing, and connecting information part of your life.

Here's a typical example from my own life of the kind of accidental way most people pick up information. In May 1978, I attended the National Stationery Show in New York City because of a giftware manufacturing and distribution business I had called Distinctive Designs. I spent two days walking around asking questions and talking to dozens of people. Near the end of the show I stopped by a label manufacturing booth and started talking to the company's national sales manager. In the course of the conversation, the sales manager mentioned a new label application technology that his company was experimenting with. As I

Seeing the Pattern
Figure 3–1

listened to the salesman, it became clear—the new label was exactly what I needed to bring a decorative soap line to market. In this instance, as it happens sometimes, it didn't take much analysis. The connection occurred quickly. But if I hadn't gone to the trade show I would never have learned about the experimental label application process and most likely would not have introduced what turned out to be a very successful product. We sold almost a million bars of the decorative soap. And this valuable piece of information really came to me by accident. It is true I went to the show looking for information but at that time I didn't intellectually understand that you have to work at information gathering as hard as you work at business.

However, in business even little pieces of information can be invaluable. At Model American, shortly after we started, we talked to several Boston banks about our accounts receivable. We knew that, with our computers costing approximately $2,000 apiece, we needed accounts receivable financing if we were going to support our expected growth rate. And we knew that we'd be severely limited if we were not able to arrange the financing.

However, in the course of discussions with Federal Express we learned that it was instituting a new program that would allow us to ship computers C.O.D., and FedEx would send the customers' checks back to us overnight. This meant that, if we shipped a computer on Monday, we would have the payment by Wednesday. This little piece of information allowed sales to grow without having to establish receivables financing.

ALWAYS GATHER, PROCESS, AND CONNECT INFORMATION

Even though gathering, processing, and connecting information takes a lot of time and energy, it has to be done. And it can't be done by accident. A lot of important information comes "by accident," because you don't always know the source of the next piece of information or even what it will be. But, if you work at gathering information and do it all the time, what you will find is that more and more information will come to you "by accident." And soon you'll realize it's no longer an accident but a technique, a method. It becomes second nature to you. You'll do it regularly and you'll do it well, but you **always** have to do it.

Read in your spare time, talk to people as much as you can, go to trade shows, and so forth. Perhaps today you won't need the information but tomorrow you will. And what is not surprising is that every successful businessperson gathers, processes, and connects information all the time. In an article describing a week in Bill Gates's life, it is repeatedly mentioned that he constantly reads and enters data into his notebook computer:[2]

> Bill reads voraciously. In airports and hotels he rarely watches people, preferring to keep his eyes on newspapers, magazines or his laptop [computer].

Robert Greenberg, founder of several multimillion dollar businesses, including L.A. Gear, Inc., an athletic footwear manufacturing and marketing company,[3]

> still spends a lot of his free time watching people's feet, and he has been known to work weekends posing as a salesman at a shoe store in the Valley or wandering the terminals of LAX. "I haven't seen the last minute of a movie in seven years, because I like to be the first one out of the theater so that I can watch 300 people walk by real fast. I spot trends that way," he says.

According to their personalities and the needs of their businesses, successful businesspeople use different methods to gather, process, and connect information, but they always do it. And no wonder, they make so much money at it.

Here's another example from Greenberg's life. In the late 1970s, he opened several roller skating sales and rental stores in the Venice Beach area of Los Angeles. After doing reasonably

[2]Rich Karlgaard, "On the Road with Bill Gates," *Forbes ASAP* (Fall 1993), p. 73.
[3]David J. Jefferson, "Don't Walk a Mile in His Shoes," *Los Angeles Magazine* (December 1991), pp. 115–122.

well for a couple of years, he noticed that, in addition to coming into his stores to buy or rent skates, teenage girls were interested in buying just the laces. In fact, he was selling almost as many laces as skates. In 1982, armed with this information and a tip from his neighbor about a new movie Universal was releasing, Greenberg secured the laces licensing rights for $5,000, even though he'd never seen the film. The film was *E.T., the Extra-Terrestrial*, and the E.T.-adorned laces raked in $3 million in three months. Greenberg used that money to start L.A. Gear.

Sure, every entrepreneur is not going to turn a $5,000 investment into $3 million in three months but the principle of "gathering, processing, and connecting information" is the same. And as I said at the beginning of this chapter, gathering, processing, and connecting information is not something that only the top businesspeople in the world can do. Everyone gathers, processes, and connects information every day in different ways. When I'm in my car, occasionally I listen to sports talk shows and I'm always amazed at how expert some callers are who bet on games. These callers read newspapers from two or three major cities, subscribe to betting magazines, listen to sports shows, track team records, know who's injured and who's healthy, know whether the games are played indoors or outdoors, on artificial or natural turf, and if played outdoors, what the weather conditions are. And they don't just collect this information and leave it in a shoe box. They think about it, analyze it, connect it, and then come up with their bets.

Now, putting aside the pros and cons of gambling, I want to point out how universal the practice of gathering, processing, and connecting information is and how natural it is. From hobbies, to buying a new car, to putting a new deck on your house, to planning a vacation, we all gather, process, and connect information. But if you're building and running a business you can't do it occasionally or halfheartedly. You have to do it all the time and do it thoroughly. The rhythm of business is a continual process that goes on throughout the life of a business; and as we've seen, gathering, processing, and connecting information is a continual process that goes on throughout every step of the rhythm of business. It's not something you do while you're writing your business plan, trying to impress investors, and then forget.

"HEARING" THE INFORMATION

When I was nine years old, I started violin lessons. But before I got to hold the violin, my teacher made me listen to music. A lot of music. She wanted the music to become so much a part of me that I could "hear" the notes in my head. She believed that, if I couldn't "hear" the music, I wouldn't be able to feel the rhythm of the music. She was right. First, you have to know how to "hear" the music. In business, you have to learn how to "hear" the information so you'll know what it's telling you. Greenberg, a footwear manufacturer, looks at feet. Gates, a software developer, reads the latest books in his field as well as technical and popular newspapers and magazines. Depending on your business, you have to find your own unique sources of information. But the point is information is as basic to business as "hearing" the music is to playing the violin. And, once you understand the importance of gathering, processing, and connecting information, you can use that understanding to help you feel the rhythm of business. At first, you may be overwhelmed by the sheer volume of information but today's technologies can help you, although it wasn't always that way.

LEVELING THE DANCE FLOOR

Until the early 1980s, one of the biggest advantages the CEOs of large companies had over smaller company CEOs was their ability to use people and technology to help gather and process information. CEOs of large corporations could afford to have employees on staff whose only purpose was to gather and process information. More important, they had the use of mainframe or minicomputers. In fact, the computers and the people usually were under the direction of a specific individual whose function was devoted to information, the company's chief information officer.

Unfortunately for small businesses, even if the individuals involved appreciated the importance of information, they had to do their own gathering and processing. They couldn't afford either the extra people or the significant cost of computing power. And the pressure of daily operating issues drastically shortened the time they had to devote to the critically important task of gathering, processing, and connecting information.

All that changed because of two youthful entrepreneurs—Steve Jobs and Steve Wozniak. With the introduction of their Apple microcomputer, followed shortly by the introduction of the IBM PC, smaller companies finally had a tool that "leveled the dance floor."

Over the past 20 years, significant advances have been made to both microcomputer hardware and software. In fact, for under $2,000, any company can afford a desktop or notebook computer equivalent to yesterday's mainframe. When it is used in conjunction with the other information tools available—cellular phones, fax modems, palmtop computers, video conferencing, personal digital assistants, and the like—today's businessperson is well equipped to do battle.

And it's not just all the fancy hardware that is changing how business is done. To make all these technological toys useful, there are thousands of powerful software programs, on-line services, and the cyberspace of the global Internet and the World Wide Web. For example, when groupware or Internet software is put on a company microcomputer network, the result is like a giant brain. And the Internet makes it possible for people to work with one another and share information and knowledge without worrying about location or time. It's clear that you're a lot smarter with your microcomputer than you are without it.

In short, to have a successful business you have to feel the rhythm of business, and information is one of the basic beats of that rhythm, because information is part of every step. When you're looking for a marketplace opportunity, you have to gather, process, and connect information. When you're developing a business concept to fulfill your customers' wants and needs, you have to gather, process, and connect information. When you're interacting with customers, you have to gather, process, and connect information. And when you step back to analyze and refine your product or service and your business concept, you have to gather, process, and connect information. So, there's no getting around it. Information is vital to every step in the rhythm of business.

KEY POINTS IN CHAPTER 3

• To feel the rhythm of business, you must understand the importance of information and realize that it isn't so much a word or a revolution as a technique.

• The value of information comes when you gather, process, and connect it.

• When it comes to information, you can't rely on accidents or be lazy in your thinking. You have to make gathering, processing, and connecting information part of your business life.

• According to their personalities and the needs of their businesses, successful businesspeople use different methods to gather, process, and connect information, but they always do it.

• The rhythm of business is a continual process that goes on throughout the life of a business, and as we've seen, gathering, processing, and connecting information is a continual process that goes on throughout every step of the rhythm of business.

Choose a job you love,
and you will never have to
work a day in your life.
…CONFUCIUS

4

Love and Passion

No, you haven't picked up the wrong book. I know that "Love and Passion" sounds like the title of a romance novel. **But if you want to be successful, you must love the business you are in with a passion**.

Why is loving the business you are in with a passion so important? Starting and running a successful business takes a huge emotional commitment. If you are one of the lucky ones with an inborn ability to feel the rhythm of business, you implicitly understand the emotional commitment you have to make to your business. You know all too well that running a business is not an eight-hour a day, five-day a week commitment.

Contrary to popular belief, being a success in business is not about belonging to exclusive country clubs, driving Cadillacs, and owning your own yacht. In fact, it's not even about jobs and careers, because you might very well change jobs and careers several times throughout your working days. Being a successful businessperson is really a way of being. It's who you are.

And being a success in business is really about doing what you love, because business requires a commitment 24 hours a day, 7 days a week, 365 days a year, year-in and year-out. There are no vacations, no sick days and no personal days. Sure, you're not physically "in the office" all that time, but you are thinking about your business all the time. There is no way to "punch out" and go home. Besides, you don't want to—you love it! And your love for your business gives you the drive you need to maintain that type of commitment. It simply isn't enough to enjoy or like the business you're in. If you do not love your business, you will not be able to give your business the time, energy, thought, and emotion it needs to become successful.

In Chapter 2, I said that, to build and run a business, you must identify a business concept able to provide your customers with exactly what they want and need. This means that really your customers and their wants and needs determine what your business does and how it does it. Now, I'm saying that you also must love your business. Putting these two statements together, you build a successful business (as shown in Figure 4–1) by giving your customers what they want and need while doing what you love.

When you're thinking about what business would best allow you to satisfy your customers, you also have to ask yourself whether you'll love being in that business. If the answer is no, don't kid yourself. Don't be in that business. It probably won't be successful and you won't be happy. Even if you're thinking about joining a company that is already up and running, you want to make sure that it is in a field you love. As sappy as it sounds, love is a magic ingredient that allows you to work harder with less strain and allows you to learn more with less effort and leads directly to business success. If you read the stories of successful businesspeople, the most common ingredient is that they all love the businesses they are in.

Choosing a business is a lot like choosing a spouse. There's no guarantee that, even if you love your prospective spouse, the marriage will be successful, but it's foolish to agree to marry someone you don't love in the hope that you'll grow to love that person. A marriage is almost never successful if you don't love your spouse when you get married. And it's the same in business:

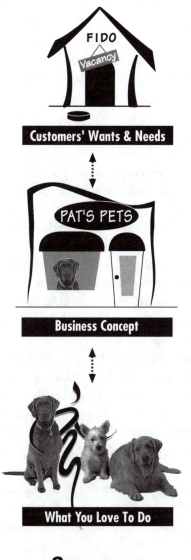

Success

Figure 4–1

If you don't love it, don't be in it. It won't work out. Of course, it might happen that after five years, even though you once loved the business, you now hate it. Then, that's the time to get out. There's no guarantee that you'll always love the business you're in just like there's no guarantee that you'll always love your spouse (the divorce rate in the United States is over 50 percent). But, at least, you should give yourself a chance by starting out in a business you love.

PASSION FOR THE DANCE

We began this chapter mentioning the amount of time a business requires and that commitment cannot be underestimated. If you go into a coffeehouse anywhere in America, you're likely to find some scruffy-haired folk singer standing at a mike with a guitar wailing out a song about the working man (or woman). But at five o'clock when the whistle blows, that "underpaid, overworked, sweaty-browed working man" goes home and he doesn't show up again till he's due in at eight. On weekends, he doesn't show up at all. And he doesn't think about business when he's watering his lawn. Why should he? He's home.

But as someone who's striving for business success, **you** work late, show up early, work weekends, and think about your business all the time. Why? It's not just because you have good stock options. You are in a business you love so much you don't want to do anything else. And, if you own the business, you must have even more devotion. After all, your name is on the bank loans. Your home is at risk. Your family is counting on the business to be a success. If you don't love your business, all that time, effort, and risk aren't worth it. From sales to manufacturing, from financing to advertising, from hiring to firing, from managing to negotiating, from analyzing to planning—as an entrepreneur you have to do it all, or at the very least, see that it all gets done and done right.

There's never any letup. It's not as if a business takes a lot of work when it's a startup and then you can slack off when it's a success. I've mentioned over and over that business is a rhythm, a process. That rhythm, that process doesn't end, it just keeps rolling along. Customers' wants and needs are always changing. The means to fulfill those wants and needs are always changing. Competitors are always nipping at your heels. Every business has to keep bringing its product or service to the market, analyzing the results, and changing the product or service to come closer and closer to fulfilling its customers' wants and needs.

The more successful a company is, the more work it takes. The difference between a company of one and a company of a thousand is that in a company of a thousand, there are a thousand more things to worry about. Of course, when a business is successful, the founder(s) can always choose to retire or quit, but as long as the founder(s) stay in the game, running a business is a full-time commitment.

And to give a business the time it requires, you have to have the energy to support that commitment, which is why you must love your business with a passion. If you love your business, that love makes your energy flow. Getting up in the morning is something you look forward to. Once you get to work, the hours fly by. On the other hand, if you don't love your business, mornings are a torture. Every afternoon is a drudgery. And you simply lack the stamina to make the business a success. You want to be anywhere except in your office. You find that you're always battling fatigue, colds, and other health-related problems. Doing something you don't like for too long is a mental and physical strain that simply is going to harm you and all those around you. So, love your business or get out of it.

THE ROLLER COASTER RIDE OF BUSINESS

Do you remember the first time you built up enough courage to get on a roller coaster? You couldn't wait for it to start. No matter how much you heard about what it was like and no matter how many times you watched others go on the ride, nothing prepared you for how you felt as the car started up that first incline. Once at the peak, nothing prepared you for how quickly you were headed for the bottom. What had been a slow, enjoyable ride became a terrifying, heart-pounding rush. And, just as you bottomed out and your heart slowed to a more normal beat, you were once again heading upward, reaching for the sky. Remember, when you got off that roller coaster, you said to yourself, "That was great! I loved it! I can't wait to get back on."

Welcome to the world of business. Your emotional highs and lows on the road to success are very much like that roller coaster ride. Take a look at Figure 4–2. The process of building and running a business is an experience that is filled with the highest highs and the lowest lows. And like a real roller coaster, the highs and lows are not separated by months, weeks, or even days. The highs and lows can shift in a matter of minutes or seconds.

A good example of how quickly emotions can change happened to me at Distinctive Designs, my giftware manufacturing and distribution company. I spent three months during 1981 courting a Japanese stationery manufacturer for the exclusive distribution rights for the United States for a new line of children's stationery it had introduced. The Christmas selling season was approaching and the president of the company kept delaying his answer. I had gotten to the point where I was convinced my firm would not get the contract and would lose the entire Christmas selling season. Needless to say, I was not very happy. My happiness sank into depression when, over the weekend, I got a call from my contact in Japan, who indicated that the president was going to say no. I can remember clearly sitting in my office that Monday, looking out the window at a beautiful Fall day, wondering if I was going to have to sell my house to stay in business. Then, the phone rang. The president of the Japanese firm informed me that he had decided to give my company the distributorship and requested I come to Japan to sign the agreement. My contact wasn't wrong. The president had changed his mind over the weekend and my depression turned to euphoria.

The Emotional Roller Coaster

Figure 4–2

That's how the roller coaster goes: up and down, up and down. So, it's important to love the business you're in because it's always easy to stay on the roller coaster when it's going up but it's a lot harder when it's going down. However, that's when it's most important to stay on, and your love and passion for your business will keep you on the ride. And not only do you have to stay on the ride but everyone involved in the business has to stay along on the ride. The highs and lows of the business are not going to be felt just by you. Employees feel them. Customers feel them. Suppliers feel them. Financial backers feel them. And your family certainly feels them.

When something good happens, everyone involved in the business is going to be happy. When something bad happens, everyone involved in the business is going to be unhappy. Then it's your love, your enthusiasm, your passion for your business that helps keep up everyone's spirits. You have to keep everyone working hard; the business's backers from losing faith; the customers from going away; the employees from quitting; your family from urging you to give up. Your emotional commitment to your business drives the business; and the more deeply you feel it, the more deeply you'll make others feel it. For example, when Bill Gates talks about how he gets people excited about Microsoft, he often responds, "I paint a picture of excitement because this is what I feel."[1] Gates's love for his business enables him to paint the picture that in turn excites customers, employees, and investors about working with or investing in Microsoft.

LOVE AND RHYTHM

But the most important reason for loving your business is because love really makes the rhythm of business come alive. The more you love your business, the closer you'll be to its heart, its pulse, its essence. These, perhaps, are abstract, "romanticized" words to use for a book on business but "feeling" the rhythm of

[1]"Tycoon," *NBC News* (May 26, 1995).

business goes beyond words, so you have to use a method of feeling the rhythm of business that also goes beyond words. That something is love. Love goes beyond words. It doesn't matter whether we're talking about love for another person, or art, or business. When love grows, we begin to develop an intuitive understanding that exists on a feeling level. When married, we develop an intuitive understanding about our wife or husband or children because of our love. Artists develop an intuitive understanding of their work because of their love. In the same way, when running a business, if you love it, you develop an intuitive understanding about it because of your love. When you love your business, you learn to feel what your business needs. You learn to feel when everything is okay or when something's wrong. You learn to feel when customers are happy and when employees are happy. You learn to feel when a decision is right and when it's a mistake. You learn to feel when it's time to enter a market and when it's time to leave. And that kind of feeling only comes from practical experience and from love.

In Chapter 3, I discussed what increases your understanding during each step of a customer interaction cycle. And it's information. Frankly, when you're at your office, handling day-to-day business affairs, you probably have no time to make the kind of use of information that your business needs. Sure, you give directions, meet with customers and suppliers, make speeches, and do all the other tasks your business requires, but those tasks most often demand a superficial kind of thinking. The type of creative thinking that is really important occurs at the beginning or end of the day, when you're alone at your desk or in the quiet of your car or when you're sitting at home or lying in bed before you fall asleep. In that silence, you think long, hard, and deep and ask yourself the important questions about your business. Are you really satisfying your customers' wants and needs? Are you really producing your product or service in the most efficient way possible? Are you really marketing your product or service in the most effective way possible? Indeed, this is when you not only think about your business, you **feel** your business. This is when the rhythm of business sings to your soul, because this is when the information you were too busy to think about during the day bubbles up in your mind. This is when information you don't even know you have comes to you and connects together. But the simple fact is, if you don't love your business, these connections, ideas, feelings, and rhythm never will come to you because as soon as you're out of the office, you won't want to think about your business. In your quiet times, you'll think about everything but your business. But if you love your business, your quiet times will always be filled with thoughts of your business.

Here's an example of what I mean from Robert Greenberg. When Greenberg used the money he made selling the E.T. adorned laces to open a 6,500-square-foot clothing store on Los Angeles's Melrose Avenue in 1983, he knew how important it was for him to come up with the right name for the store. But how did the name come to him? As he tells it:[2]

> A woman selling T-shirts came into the company's warehouse downtown and, laying them out for an employee, said, "This is real L.A. gear." The employee scrawled down the name and submitted it for a contest I was having to name the store. Of course, I looked at the piece of paper and threw it away. But at 4 in the morning, I woke up and thought, My God, **L.A. Gear!**

And that's how the company got its name. You might say it was just a "lucky" accident but it's not. It happened because Greenberg loved his business and somewhere deep down he was always thinking about his business, so at 4 A.M., when all the chatter in his mind quieted, suddenly what he had read and was right but at the time was too busy to process popped up— L.A. Gear. At 4 A.M.! In the middle of the night, his mind processed the information, saw the pattern, and made the right connection. As it turned out, the L.A. Gear name was instrumental to his company's success. But that experience is not something you practice, it's not something you go to school and learn. This

2Jefferson, 1991, p. 117.

type of quiet thinking can't be forced or programmed, it's either there or it isn't. If you love your business, it's there; and thus the channel for new connections, new ideas, new feelings always is open. If you don't love your business, new ideas, new connections, new feelings may come to you occasionally, but eight hours a day, five days a week in the office simply doesn't provide enough time, and certainly not enough quiet thinking time. But the more you love your business, the more you will think about your business and the more these experiences will occur. Like Robert Greenberg, gradually, you will attune yourself to the rhythm of business and you'll find the right connections clicking together in your mind more and more. You will improve your ability to "see" the patterns. You will increase your understanding of your customers' wants and needs and the business concept best able to satisfy those wants and needs, and you will move your business closer and closer to that unreachable but always alluring goal of the ideal business.

SIX INGREDIENTS FOR FEELING THE RHYTHM OF BUSINESS

As I said at the beginning of this book, learning to feel the rhythm of business is a combination of six things: having some basic business skills, working hard and practicing, understanding the basic mechanics of your business, gathering information about your business, thinking about your business, and loving your business with a passion. But the true key to learning how to feel the rhythm of business is loving your business. If you love your business, everything else will fall into place. If you love your business, you must have some skills at it, you'll work hard and practice to develop even more skills, you'll strive to deepen your understanding of your business, you'll continually gather information about your business, and in your quiet times, you'll constantly think about your business and then, gradually, through the combination of all six ingredients, you will attune yourself to the rhythm of business. Some people are more intuitive than others but everyone's intuition can grow, and the growth of intuition is based on love. Learning to feel the rhythm of business is a natural process, but by having an intellectual grasp of the process, it can be helped along. Be in a business that you love, and once you're in the business, constantly work hard at it, constantly seek to understand it, constantly gather information about it, constantly think about it, and soon you'll find that you are feeling its rhythm.

RHYTHM IS NOT A METAPHOR

The rhythm of business is not something mystical and magical. It is not a theory or a catchy metaphor thrown out to sound good. The rhythm of business is the continuous flow of one customer interaction cycle after another, and the most important aspect of feeling the rhythm is that it helps you not only understand each step but the timing of when you must move between steps—when it's right to stop planning and start preparing, when it's time to stop preparing and start interacting, when it's right to stop interacting and start analyzing and refining, and when it's right to stop analyzing and refining and start another customer interaction cycle and then another and another. Understanding this flow—feeling this timing—is the combination of information and love. That is how you "feel" when it is right to move from step to step and from cycle to cycle. That is the real rhythm of business, and developing skill at it comes from the practical experience of being in business (which provides the information) and loving the business you are in (which obviously provides the love).

Again, there is a parallel to romance. You might think of yourself as a romantic person but only when you **actually** fall in love does abstract love flame into passion because then the experience of a real relationship makes your heart grow. It is the same with business. You might love the idea of being in business but only when you actually **are** in business will your abstract love flame into passion. Thus, your passion combined with your experience makes your intuition grow. So, even though this is a book about business, although it might sound corny, it is a romance because it's also about love.

KEY POINTS IN CHAPTER 4

• If you want to be successful, you must love the business you are in with a passion.

• Being a successful businessperson is really a way of being. It's who you are.

• If you do not love your business, you will not be able to give your business the time, energy, thought, and emotion it needs to become successful.

• You build a successful business by giving your customers what they want and need while doing what you love.

• The process of building and running a business is an experience filled with the highest highs and the lowest lows.

• Your emotional commitment to your business drives the business; and the more deeply you feel it, the more deeply you'll make others feel it.

• The most important creative thinking usually occurs at the beginning or end of the day when you're alone at your desk or in the quiet of your car or when you're sitting at home or lying in bed before falling asleep. In that silence, you think long, hard, and deep and ask yourself the important questions about your business.

• The true key to learning how to feel the rhythm of business is loving your business. If you love your business, everything else will fall into place. If you love your business, you must have some skill at it, you'll work hard and practice to develop even more skill, you'll strive to deepen your understanding of your business, you'll continually gather information about your business, and in your quiet times, you'll constantly think about your business and then, gradually, through the combination of all six ingredients, you will attune yourself to the rhythm of business.

Part II

*Learning to Feel
the Rhythm*

The secret of success in life is to be ready for opportunity when it comes.

...BENJAMIN DISRAELI

5

The Customer Always Leads

The rhythm of business is dominated by a customer orientation because customers drive business. As we saw in Chapter 2, the rhythm of business begins with the identification of an opportunity in the marketplace. In that chapter, we discussed briefly that you should look for business opportunities in areas with which you are familiar, such as your hobbies or work experience. Familiarity brings with it knowledge, and when you are in a business you need as much knowledge as you can get. But knowledge is not the same as ideas. If you want to start or run a business, how do you get your ideas and how do you know if the ideas are any good?

Actually, although ideas for businesses are not as easy to come by as knowledge (you can't buy an encyclopedia of business ideas) you might be surprised to hear that we all get good ideas for businesses all the time. For example, how many times have you said to yourself, "I bet I could make a million dollars if I made this or sold that." It's a very common thought because we're all customers, and if at work or at home, we find ourselves wanting or needing some product or service, the idea naturally occurs that we could make a lot of money providing that same product or service to other people. Whether it's a new wrench or a better delivery service or a spicier tomato juice, the logic is persuasive: if I have a want or need, others probably have the same want or need, and many successful businesses and new product or service launches are begun by just such logic but, unfortunately, many more remain only ideas.

Why? One reason is that most business ideas do not stand up to practical scrutiny. They require hard-to-get resources or skills we lack or use technology that doesn't yet exist. But even dismissing the vast majority of impractical ideas, many business ideas come back to us again and again and seem good every time. Yet, we still don't act. Why? It is due to three main reasons: lack of knowledge, unwillingness to expend the energy, and fear of the risk involved.

Knowledge can be learned from books, working with those more experienced and skilled, and taking business courses. The energy comes from being in a business you love. But how do you overcome the risk? For most, the risks of starting a new business or launching a new project are very intimidating, which is why understanding the rhythm of business is so important. **Understanding the rhythm of business and following it lessens the risks associated with being in business**.

Clearly, this is a very important point, and it will help you through every step in the rhythm of business. However, as we are beginning this chapter with a discussion of how to come up with and evaluate good business ideas, let's see how understanding the rhythm of business helps in identifying valid business opportunities.

ALL IDEAS NEED A CUSTOMER FOCUS

As the rhythm of business is based on the customer, all ideas should have a customer focus. For instance, we just discussed that one good way of getting business ideas is by using ourselves as a customer. It's a common starting point because we all understand ourselves, and if we could truly know that what pleased us pleased others, we would stand a very good chance of making a lot of money. So, not surprisingly, this model for success is followed by many businesspeople.

Paul Hawken, a gardening enthusiast, started Smith & Hawken, a successful mail-order and retail store business, because for years he could never find the right gardening tools. He wanted high-quality, reasonably priced, specialized tools that weren't available in hardware and gardening stores. After investigating the industry and talking to other hobbyists, he concluded that here was an opportunity for a business and began providing high-quality, competitively priced tools for the "serious" gardening hobbyist.

Scott Cook, the founder of Intuit, Inc., created Quicken, the best-selling home and small business financial software package, when his wife complained that doing the family bills was too time-consuming and difficult. Scott figured that, if his wife, a computer-marketing consultant with an M.B.A. degree, found the available accounting software much too complex, lots of other people must feel that way, too. Scott concluded that, if he developed a simple software product based on the metaphor of a checkbook, something that everyone was familiar with, he would have a winner. He was right. Within a month of introduction, Intuit's product "blew away the competition."

Starbucks's Howard Schultz was ambling through a piazza in Milan, noting with approval the Italians' fondness for cafes that served up good coffee and good conversation.[1] He rued that there was nothing like it in America. Then he thought, maybe there should be. American alcohol consumption was falling, but the American love for coffee was holding strong. Maybe Americans would go for Italian-style coffee bars. When this idea connected, Mr. Schultz recalls, "It was Nirvana."

---

[1]Brent Bowers and Udayian Gupta, "New Entrepreneurs Offer a Simple Lesson in Building a Fortune," *Wall Street Journal* (October 19, 1994), p. A13.

As you can see, Paul Hawken, Scott Cook, and Howard Schultz developed successful business opportunities based on their own wants and needs. Perhaps, not all businesses are started this way but very many are. What is similar about each is that it involves an area the individual is familiar with and where the customer is someone like oneself. Paul Hawken is a businessman and a serious gardener. Scott Cook is a computer programmer making an accounting program for his wife. Howard Schultz is a businessman and a coffee lover. So, all three have the knowledge and the love to pursue their ideas and each knows his customer intimately.

A RESTAURANT ISN'T JUST A GREAT CHEF

However, let me note here a mistake a lot of people make when looking for a business opportunity. They think merely by having a great deal of expertise in a field they can lower the risk associated with being in that business. Obviously, knowledge of a field indeed is a help in running a successful business, but as Michael Gerber, author of the *E-Myth*, points out, "The technical work of a business and a business that does that technical work are two totally different things!"[2] Just because you are a great chef does not necessarily mean you can run a successful restaurant. You have to love the business you're in, but to be a success in business you also have to love business. A restaurant is not only about great food. It also involves marketing, accounting, decorating, managing, and above all, knowing your customers and fulfilling their wants and needs, not yours. All too often, technical experts open a business in their field to fill their own desires not their customers', which is why you have to love business. **Business is about satisfying customers. Business is not about satisfying the egos of those in business.** Even though that point is basic, it's forgotten over and over again, and not just by those starting out in business. Large, established companies forget it, too.

[2]Michael E. Gerber, *The E Myth* (Cambridge, Mass.: Ballinger, 1986).

For example, in the early 1990s, Honda's sales slumped. Commenting on the decline, CEO Nobuhiko Kawamoto said in *Fortune* magazine,[3] "The traditions that guarded this company for 40 years weren't functioning properly. Our focus on the customer was vague." According to Kawamoto, the company had become too focused on engineering. Always a pride for the company, engineering goals became too important. Kawamoto said, "the engineers became diverted by their own goals and produced cars that were hard to build, cost too much and didn't click with buyers." In other words, Honda's engineers were making cars to please themselves, not their customers. Of course, Honda's engineers thought they were customer focused because they were turning out well-engineered cars. But they didn't really know their customers, who desired fewer engineering frills and were eager for better pricing and styling.

IS THERE A PAYING CUSTOMER?

Business is more than expertise in a field. Business is a process, and that process always requires a focus on the customer. However, as you can see from the examples of Hawken, Cook, and Schultz, the ideas that begin the process of business are not necessarily extraordinary or require a special type of genius. One way or another, we all have good ideas for starting companies or developing new products and services. But our idea must fulfill the wants and needs of customers. And that leads us to the million-dollar question: How do you know when an idea will please the wants and needs of customers? And the million-dollar answer is, "You don't know." No one knows. But if you understand the rhythm of business, you know the way to find out—plan the idea, test the idea in the marketplace, analyze and refine the idea, and then reenter the marketplace with a better understanding of what your customer truly wants and needs. And then repeat this cycle over and over, because customers, markets,

[3] Alex Taylor III, "The Man Who Put Honda Back on Track," *Fortune* (September 9, 1996), pp. 92–100.

and technologies always change and your company must change with them. In the world of business, the most important question for any product or service must always be, **"Is there a customer willing to pay money for this product or service?"** It's such a simple and obvious point, but many people invest large amounts of money in new and old businesses without knowing this vital fact. They might have thought they knew but, in reality, they had the wrong product or the wrong price or the wrong marketing campaign, and they never bothered to validate their assumptions in the real world with real customers. Even if you start with yourself as a customer, that's not good enough. **You must always learn as much as you can about your paying customers and their wants and needs.** Your own wants and needs may not be typical for reasons you don't suspect but must find out.

Much to my own chagrin, I am an example of this classic mistake. In 1986, I was part of a team that designed a financial planning software product. Using ourselves as customers, we identified a marketplace opportunity as entrepreneurs who needed "to prepare financial projections quickly and inexpensively," and further, we divided those entrepreneurs into two categories: startup entrepreneurs and small business owners. Since we knew it was impossible to get a bank or individual to invest in a business without first seeing the company's financial projections, we felt that every entrepreneur would want to know how to calculate and understand the financial implications of his or her business ideas and decisions. We concluded that an easy-to-use software product that provided those capabilities would be a sure winner, and in our supreme confidence, we started the company. Financing was raised from a group of wealthy individual investors whom we managed to convince by our enthusiasm and track record as businessmen, which is a warning to all potential investors. No matter how good a team's track record or how convincing its enthusiasm, make sure the team really knows its customers.

Then, we developed our product. After more than 18 months and almost $2 million had been raised and spent, with great fanfare, we introduced our financial planning software. However, it didn't take long to realize something was wrong. Although the software won awards at software industry shows and was widely acclaimed in the business press, we weren't getting the customers—the product simply wasn't selling at retail outlets. After much agonizing analysis, we realized we had misjudged our customer. It wasn't that our target customers, entrepreneurs and small business owners, didn't need our product. They did. But, for the most part, they simply didn't know they needed it. And worse, once it was pointed out to them by a banker or potential investor that, in fact, they did have to prepare detailed financial projections, instead of running out to buy our product or even a competitive product, they chose to have the work done by an accountant or business consultant. Apparently, it didn't matter to them that they didn't understand the financial implications of their business ideas and decisions.

We concluded that, instead of going after entrepreneurs and small business owners, we should target the advisors and consultants. In essence, our goal of empowering entrepreneurs to take control of their financial decisions, although worthwhile, wasn't attainable based on real customer wants and needs. Once we locked onto our new target customer and showed a few our product, they loved it. But now we were faced with having to rework the software to eliminate some of its less sophisticated elements and to raise more money to fund a new marketing campaign. However, as you can imagine, raising money to make changes in a company that has already encountered difficulty is a lot harder than raising money for a new company. As a result, we had to scale back our plans significantly.

Obviously, along the way we made many assumptions that contributed to our precarious situation. But, more than any other, our erroneous assumptions regarding our customers created the company's problems. And it resulted from having such supreme confidence in what we thought we knew that we didn't feel it necessary to increase our understanding of who our customers **really** were and what they **really** wanted. We were right in using ourselves as customers to develop the seed idea for our business but we were wrong in not validating our idea. As impossible as it seems to me now, we invested our own money and others in a guess—a wrong guess! Yet we were so confident we didn't even think of the risk. But you must always think of the risk and how to lower it—and the best way to lower it is by knowing your customers through real customer interactions.

However, even though we totally misjudged our target customer, our company still could have survived relatively unscathed if back then, we had understood the rhythm of business and planned for the possibility of failure, if we had planned for the possibility of change, if we had kept enough capital in reserve for just such contingencies. Remember, no one can plan a perfect business. Even with sufficient test marketing, adjustments have to be made. If we had kept enough capital in reserve, our first launch of our business, while large and extravagant, would merely have been our first customer interaction cycle. By cycle 2, we would have locked onto our real customer, and instead of having a major crisis, we would have had a costly but manageable blip in a beginning business. Unfortunately, back then I didn't know the rhythm of business, although the experience was one of the hard lessons that taught me the rhythm of business. However, I am happy to say that, through the sheer determination of two of the founding team and much of their own money, this company has survived. And recently, the company introduced a Windows version of its product and is hopeful that that product may yet realize the company's original growth and profitability objectives.

VALUE DELIVERED

But now that I've shown the wrong way to grow a business, let's take a detailed look at Tim DeMello, an experienced businessperson who I feel has an instinctive understanding of the rhythm of business and see how he is going about the business building process. Tim was a stockbroker for six years before he quit his job and developed the popular AT&T Investment Challenge, which he later sold for nearly $2 million. But the company we will look at in this book is Tim's second business, Streamline, Inc.

Tim DeMello originally got the idea for his second business when he was starting his first. Under the stress and time pressure of being part of a dual-wage earning family, simple basics such as shopping for food and clothes had become major undertakings. After selling his first business, DeMello remembered how often he and his wife had wished for an easier way to get the shopping done. With so many other couples involved in dual careers, Tim guessed he and many of his friends were not the only ones with the same wish. Thus, in his own family's wants and needs, Tim felt he saw an opportunity for a business. The convergence of two major trends—changes in lifestyles, resulting in increased pressures on individuals, plus the movement of technology into the home with computers, cable TV, and faxes—Tim believed, was creating a significant marketplace opportunity for home delivery businesses.

In this way, the idea for Streamline was born. As expressed by Tim's mission statement Streamline's goal is[4]

> To be recognized as a leading consumer services company through innovative ideas and superior service. Streamline plans to provide products, services, and information to the home for the convenience of today's consumers who place a high value on their time and demand product quality and service excellence. The Company plans to consolidate a wide variety of necessity-based consumable, disposable or renewable products and services, currently purchased by consumers from multiple retailers and suppliers, and deliver them directly to the home from its Customer Resource Centers.

Thinking of his predicament as a consumer, Tim realized such a company would have been the answer to his family's

---

[4]The information about Tim DeMello and Streamline used throughout this book is based on (1) numerous conversations with Tim and (2) several of Streamline's business plans.

dream. But to Tim, as an experienced businessman with a natural-born rhythm, his real question was this: Did a similar need exist in the marketplace of sufficient size to warrant starting such an endeavor? Because Tim had always wanted to be in a consumer-oriented business, he decided to find out. Here's what he did.

First, he spent a few weekends letting the idea percolate in his head. He thought about the proposed business from different angles, imagining if he and people he knew would really pay money for such services and what kind of services they would like. Then, he talked over the idea with his family and a few close friends to see what they thought and what kind of products and services they might suggest. He read articles on the emerging trends toward convenience shopping. He went to his local bookstore and bought books that dealt with the problems faced by dual career families and he also talked to some people who were in home delivery businesses. After about a year of informal information gathering, one morning he sat down and wrote the mission statement I quoted and began a serious investigation into starting his business. As someone who had sold a business for a couple of million dollars, Tim was in the position to form a corporation and open a small office. Others who want to start a business might have to begin part-time or borrow money but **the key is not how much money you have, it's how well you know your customers.**

This same process is true even if you are already in business and want to launch a new product or service or change an existing one. The differences are in the amount of resources you have and the scale of the operation. Of course, these are key differences that affect your flexibility and timing: The larger your company, the harder it is to respond quickly to changes in your customers' wants and needs, which is an important reason why so many large corporations are downsizing and breaking into autonomous units. But the process, the rhythm is the same. Someone perceives an opportunity due to a change in customer wants and needs or an emerging want and need and has an idea of how to fill it.

Tim, to better understand his perceived opportur
ducted a series of focus groups with area residents. H
Tim felt that, even though focus groups were a good suurce or
information as to the products consumers **might** buy, they were
limited in value because the consumers were only asked their
opinions and not required to make actual purchases. Nonetheless, Tim felt the information was valuable and later used it as
the basis for a series of real-life tests.

While he was involved in the focus groups, Tim continued
gathering information related to home delivery services. Included
in this process, Tim read hundreds of magazines and newspapers,
searched electronic databases, news retrieval services, and retail
industry analysts' reports; he even paid thousands of dollars for a
comprehensive, nationwide database on individual households
and their purchasing habits by product category.

After analyzing all this information, Tim felt he was ready
to interact with some "real" customers. He designed a mul-
tiphase, customer-based marketing test to increase his level of
knowledge of his potential customers' actual purchasing habits.
The participants chosen were located in various towns close to
the company's small office, making it efficient and cost effective
to serve them. Also, the customers chosen had demographic
profiles similar to customers in other potential sales territories.

This multicycled testing was used to:

- Provide the company with information that helped to
  define a more precise profile of the target customer.
- Prove the viability of the opportunity—that there was a
  demand and willingness to purchase products and services
  through a home delivery service.
- Determine the specific products and services that customers were likely to purchase.
- Determine if acceptable profit margins could be obtained
  for the products and services offered.
- Determine the commitment level that customers had with
  their existing vendors.

Of course, Tim didn't consciously know about the rhythm of business at this time but as a businessperson with a natural-born rhythm, Tim's exploration of the market opportunity closely follows what I've described as the rhythm of business. As it turns out, what Tim thought of as market tests wound up taking four customer interaction cycles (i.e., going through steps 1–4 four times) over a 33-month period. However, not until Tim was planning his fourth round did he come to me as a potential investor and we talked about his business. I was impressed by Tim and even more by his business plan. In fact, I was so impressed I became an investor and Tim invited me to join his Advisory Board. But you should know all of the examples I use from Tim in this book occurred before we ever discussed the rhythm of business. When Tim started his business, he was using his instincts, his experience, and his own business knowledge.

In early 1994, Tim began what I call his first customer inter-action cycle with one service to approximately 50 customers. That cycle lasted approximately two months. After carefully studying customer feedback, Tim designed cycle 2 to learn how best to combine multiple products and services and how best to deliver them into the home. Because cycle 2 focused more on the mechanics of the delivery side of his business, Tim chose to run cycle 2 using only one test customer (himself) for approximately two months. As was done after cycle 1, Tim carefully evaluated the information provided by this test and used the resulting insight to help him design his next customer interaction cycle. Cycle 3 was based on offering multiple products and services to six customers.

After cycle 3, Tim reached a critical point in the development of his business. He felt he had a good sense of the right mix of products and services and an efficient way to deliver them. But he wasn't sure whether his level of understanding had increased to the point where he was confident enough to formally launch his business.

His instincts urged him to carry out one more test cycle. Consequently, cycle 4 was structured on a larger scale, using 100 customers, offering the mix of products and services based on customer feedback from cycle 3. At the conclusion of cycle 4, Tim believed he had increased his understanding of his customers to the level where he felt there was a strong enough market to warrant moving beyond the initial test phase; and Tim opened Streamline's prototype Customer Resource Center. According to Tim, the opening of the prototype center began his fifth test cycle and would last about 15 months. The 15-month period would be used to carefully work out all of the issues associated with operating a Customer Resource Center as Streamline built its customer base to an anticipated level of 2,000 households.

We can see that, at the time Tim first identified his marketplace opportunity, he had a general understanding of his target customers based on his own wants and needs. But Tim knew he still needed to determine how broad a market was out there and if his own wants and needs indeed were typical of this much larger market. For example, from Tim's first test cycle, he discovered that his initial estimate of the products and services his customers wanted was far too limited. Based on what his customers told him, Tim decided to add several products and services, such as bottled water and photo processing and supplies, that he never would have thought to include. By the time he had reached cycle 4, Tim had added several other products and services, such as cut flowers and plants and pet food and supplies. As Tim's understanding of his customers increased, the sales potential of his business increased, which again shows that, from the moment you identify a marketplace opportunity, you must begin systematically gathering, processing, and connecting information about your **real**—not imagined—customers. How else can you lower the risks associated with business?

From Tim's first four customer interaction cycles, it's easy to see how Tim had the confidence to considerably increase his investment in his company for its major expansion in cycle 5. Tim had the knowledge that **real customers** were willing to spend **real money** for his business's products and services. Obviously, even four customer interaction cycles do not guarantee success, but contrast Tim's methods with what happened in the software business I was involved in. Think how much better off we would have been if we had tried a few small customer inter-action cycles with, perhaps, an early beta version of our soft-ware. We would have locked onto our real customers almost immediately and saved hundreds of thousands of dollars and perhaps have quickly grown our company into a multimillion-dollar business.

Never forget the secret of business success: **The more you know about your customers and their wants and needs, the easier it is to build a business that satisfies those wants and needs better than anyone else in the world**.

Guesses, friends, estimates, surveys, and focus groups are okay. They are part of every business's research tools; but before you sign away the mortgage to your house, you must base your business on real wants and needs learned from real interactions with real customers. Then, following the rhythm of business, you build from there.

WHAT IT MEANS TO UNDERSTAND YOUR CUSTOMERS

Now that we've discussed how understanding customers is the key to identifying marketplace opportunities and how that understanding lowers risk, I'd like to talk about some of the changes that have occurred and are occurring in what it means to understand your customers.

Back in the 1910s Henry Ford told his Model T customers, "You can have any color you want as long as it's black." It's not that Ford didn't realize he needed to understand and satisfy his customers. Rather, no matter how well he knew his customers, given the level of technology, his "one-size-fits-all" philosophy was all his customers could reasonably expect.

After the Second World War, technology changed, and along with it, so did customer expectations. The formula for business success shifted from "one size fits all" to choices that fit large segments of the population. You could have any color car you wanted as long as it was a model color for that year. What we had then was the mass production of products and services for large homogeneous markets. During the industrial age's mass production era, however, some businesspeople realized that they, too, could build very successful companies by focusing on the identification and satisfaction of much smaller, "niche" markets—businesses like Maaco that painted a car the exact color you wanted, no matter what year it was. These smaller niche markets were composed of customers whose desires were not being adequately addressed by the mass-produced products and services designed for larger market segments. Since that time, niche markets have proven one of the best entrees for prospective entrepreneurs.

CUSTOMIZING THE DANCE

Today, the world is vastly different than it was even a decade ago. Virtually all customers, both individual consumers and businesses, realize that they no longer need to settle for mass-produced goods and services. Instead, they expect to get exactly what they want and need—where, how, and when they want and need it—**and** get it at the right price.[5] Through advances in manufacturing and information technology, customers now know they can expect companies to cater to them as individuals. Mass customization seems like a contradiction in terms but it's true. To be successful in business today, as shown in Figure 5–1, you must see your customers as individuals, not as part of a mass market of faceless customers. Today, interactive and database technologies enable you to gather and process huge amounts of information regarding your customers. The resulting knowledge then allows your company to produce and

[5]B. Joseph Pine II, Don Peppers, and Martha Rogers, "Do You Want to Keep Your Customers Forever?" *Harvard Business Review* (March–April 1995), pp. 103–114.

Your Individual Customers
Figure 5–1

distribute **exactly** what your **individual** customers want and need, not what some broadly defined mass market wants and needs. The individually customized production of products and services already is visible today in dozens of industries, including greeting cards, supermarket delivery services, blue jeans manufacturing, and retailing services.[6] As surprising as it may seem, mass customization is showing up even in new housing developments:[7]

> Well-to-do home buyers settling in new luxury-home developments have always been able to customize their purchases, adding a greenhouse here, a bathroom there, or replacing a deck with a flagstone terrace. Now, such customization is increasingly available in developments of all price ranges as changing demographics force developers to abandon the one-size-fits-all styles of days past and build option-laden, "have it your way" tract homes.
>
> These days, developers of all sizes are not only tailoring their houses to individual tastes but are also adopting much more sophisticated sales strategies. Model homes are often outfitted to appeal to only certain demographic segments of the buying public. Advertising is targeted. Neighborhood amenities are being built with the special needs of the primary demographic group in mind.

Providing your customers with precisely what they want and need requires your business to not only know your general customer profile but to become customer intimate, gathering and processing information from each customer.[8] As much as your business allows, you need to cultivate long-term learning relationships rather than pursuing one-time transactions. And the proposition to your customer is simple—the more information the customer provides, the better able you are to provide the customer with a tailor-made solution, as shown in Figure 5–2.

---

[6]For an excellent discussion of mass customization, see B. Joseph Pine II, *Mass Customization: The New Frontier in Business Competition* (Boston: Harvard Business School Press, 1993).
[7]June Fletcher, "New Developments: Same Frames, One-of-a-Kind Frills," *Wall Street Journal* (September 8, 1995), p. B1.
[8]Pine, 1993, p. 103.

Satisfying Customers' Individual
Wants and Needs
Figure 5–2

A good example of how technology, inform
tomization are changing business can be seen
tech neighborhood pizza parlor:[9]

> Gary Mead, a trailblazer in Lompoc, California is using database
> and direct-marketing technologies to personalize his market-
> ing—and keep customers returning to Mi Amore Pizza & Pasta.
>
> The 34-year-old restaurateur's secret: a marketing database
> that tracks customers and purchases. If regulars haven't stopped
> by in 60 days, his PC-based system spits our a postcard to lure
> them back with a discount. The $10,000 system even lets him
> practice "cross-selling" techniques—such as suggesting a new
> pasta dish to pizza lovers. Every Christmas, his database cranks
> out a list of his best customers for personally signed cards. "What
> we're trying to do is establish an individual relationship with
> each customer," says Mead.
>
> Sound pie-in-the-sky? Since 1991, revenues have climbed
> more than threefold to $1 million. His delivery database now
> boasts 8,500 customers—all in a town of just 11,000. What's more,
> the delivery business is rising 25% to 30% a year.

SLOW DANCING WITH YOUR CUSTOMER

Exactly what information do you need in a customer intimate
business that you didn't know when you first identified your
marketplace opportunity? That's an important question but,
unfortunately, there is no pat answer. There are no 10 or 20
things that every business absolutely, positively has to know
about its customers other than their names and addresses and
whether they pay their bills. All the other information depends
on the nature of your specific business and the set of customer
wants and needs your business is trying to satisfy. Look at how
Stephen Silverman, an upscale clothing retailer, describes his
customer database and how effective it is for his business:[10]

[9]Gary McWilliams, "Small Fry Go Online," *Business Week*, November 20, 1995, p. 160.
[10]Stephen M. Silverman, "Retail Retold," Inc. Technology (Summer 1995), pp. 23–25.

A salesman and I are standing at the cash wrap in one of my men's clothing stores, examining a customer's purchasing history on a computer that doubles as a cash register. We carefully read the flowchart of the customer's purchasing behavior: he's bought three suits in the past year, spent more than $2,000 to date, and shopped four times in the past six months. Then we calculate the average number of times he shops in a year. That determines when the customer is likely to shop next. Should be soon, we both agree.

Next we look at the comments attached to the flowchart: The customer likes double-breasted suits and looks best in blue or gray. He favors Perry Ellis and Christian Dior suits, has one shoulder slightly lower than the other, and on his last trip to the store mentioned that he wants to buy a new suit before his wedding anniversary. Not so amazingly, we both look up to see the customer in the store at that very moment—looking at suits! The salesperson leaves my side and walks into the suit department to greet his customer personally, enthusiastically, knowledgeably. Armed with the information we've just reviewed, he is able to complete the sale—a new suit, a shirt, a tie, and suspenders—in under 15 minutes. The customer raves about how fast and easy we've made his shopping experience.

The information Stephen Silverman collects about his customers includes who they are, where they live, when they shop, how much they spend, what colors they look best wearing, and their preferences in style and designers. His database also includes information about his customer's size (i.e., a slightly lower shoulder) and comments about their future buying plans.

Now, think about Tim DeMello's business. Clearly, his database will include some of the same things such as name, address, and telephone number. But, given the different set of needs Tim's business is trying to satisfy, the top ten items in Tim's profile list include information such as whether his customers own their own homes, if they have any children or pets, if they're married, and if so, do both spouses work. In addition, Tim's list includes exactly what products and services his customers desire to purchase—groceries, health and beauty aids, bottled water, fire wood, videos, wine and beer. Also, how many weeks a year they want these products delivered and how much per week they will spend.

But regardless of what the information collected is, you need to understand that it's important to gather and process it. Stephen Silverman figures that his database represents in excess of $200,000 in business over a customer's lifetime, and if you involve your customers in educating your company about their wants and needs, your customers will be reluctant to invest additional time creating that same knowledge-based relationship with other companies. Consequently, the establishment of this mutually beneficial relationship results not only in increased sales but acts as a barrier to potential competitors. However, if your company ever ceases to provide exactly what your customers want and need, then they simply will stop doing business with you, regardless of how much time your customers have invested in your company. After all, they know that other companies are waiting to develop their own knowledge-based relationship.

So, the first step in the rhythm of business is identifying a marketplace opportunity based on the wants and needs of potential customers. And one of the best ways to identify such a marketplace opportunity is with a want or need of your own or someone you know. Then, you must reduce the risk of the opportunity by learning as much as you can about your real customers. Start small and engage in a series of low-cost, fast-paced customer interaction cycles that increase your understanding of your real customers, then design your business concept around satisfying those customers. **And, of course, what we are talking about is not just test marketing. It's planning, preparing, interacting, and analyzing and refining, which are the four steps of every customer interaction cycle.** When you start out, your interaction cycles may be small and you may think of them as what is normally considered "market tests." But what I'm saying is that, when you follow the rhythm of business, every interaction cycle is a "test," regardless of how long you've been in business or how big your business has grown. Whether you are selling one product to 50 customers or hundreds of products to tens of thousands of customers, the only difference is that more customers allow you to collect more information, so that when you analyze the results of your customer interactions, you can better refine your business to more accurately fulfill your customers' wants and needs. The four steps of a customer interaction cycle are done not just when you're starting out. These four steps never stop. They are the dance, the process, the rhythm of business. And even when your company is firmly established, you must still follow the rhythm. You must never lose sight of what your customers are telling you. You must never stop refining your business to meet your customers' changing wants and needs.

IBM IS BACK ON THE DANCE CARD

If you have any lingering doubts as to the applicability of these points to any business regardless of size, read the following from *Business Week*:[11]

> It's getting harder to remember the days when IBM was regarded as a national disaster. In the latest quarter alone, IBM snagged a staggering $11 billion in the lucrative computer-services business—winning four out of five deals it went after. . . .
>
> How did IBM achieve this turnaround?
>
> IBM has arrived at this happy juncture by doing lots of things right since chairman and Chief Executive Louis V. Gerstner Jr. took over $3\frac{1}{2}$ years ago. But the secret to IBM's success isn't great technology, cutthroat pricing, or flashy marketing moves. It's approaching double-digit growth for the first time in almost seven years for one main reason: Under Gerstner, IBM has gone back to the most basic notion of how to succeed in business: talking to customers, learning their needs, and figuring out how to satisfy them. . . .

[11]Ira Sager, "How IBM Became a Growth Company Again," *Business Week* (December 9, 1996), pp. 154–162. Reprinted with permission. © 1996 by McGraw-Hill Companies.

Gerstner's attitude is simple.

"I want to take IBM back to its roots," says Gerstner. He made it a point to get out of the office and meet regularly with customers—something his immediate predecessor John F. Akers had rarely done. By his reckoning, Gerstner still spends 40% of his time with customers, often chatting CEO to CEO, to learn what's going on.

Of course, the CEO schmooze sessions can only do so much. That's why Gerstner continues to tinker with his organization to make sure that it has the right people in the right places to maintain ties with customers and translate their requirements into products and services. . . .

. . . IBM is back on the dance card—in corporations and on Wall Street.

Clearly, Lou Gerstner is rebuilding IBM by dancing to the rhythm of business.

KEY POINTS IN CHAPTER 5

• The rhythm of business is dominated by a customer orientation because customers drive a business.

• Using oneself as a customer is a common starting point for getting ideas for businesses because we understand ourselves, and if we could truly know that what pleased us pleased others, we would stand a very good chance of making a lot of money. So, not surprisingly, this model for success is followed by many businesspeople.

• Understanding the rhythm of business and following it lessen the risks associated with being in business.

• Just because you are a great chef does not necessarily mean you can run a successful restaurant. You have to love the business you're in, but to be a success in business you also have to love business.

• Business is about satisfying customers. Business is not about satisfying the egos of those in business.

• In the world of business, the most important question for any product or service must always be, "Is there a customer willing to pay money for this product or service?"

• Never forget the secret of business success: The more you know about your customers and their wants and needs, the easier it is to build a business that satisfies those wants and needs better than anyone else in the world.

• Virtually all customers, both individual consumers and businesses, realize that they no longer need to settle for mass-produced goods and services. Instead, they expect to get exactly what they want and need—when, where, how, and at the price they want.

• To be successful in business today you must see your customers as individuals, not as part of a mass market of faceless customers.

• As much as your business allows, you need to cultivate long-term learning relationships rather than pursue one-time transactions.

• Start small and engage in a series of low-cost, fast-paced customer interaction cycles that increase your understanding of your real customers, then design your business concept around satisfying those customers. Of course, what we are talking about is **not** just test marketing. It's planning, preparing, interacting, and analyzing and refining, which are the four steps of every customer interaction cycle.

• The four steps of a customer interaction cycle are not done just when you're starting out; these four steps never stop. They are the dance, the process, the rhythm of business. And even when your company is firmly established, you still must follow the rhythm. You must never lose sight of what your customers are telling you. You must never stop refining your business to meet your customers' changing wants and needs.

Vision is the art of seeing things invisible.

...JONATHAN SWIFT

6

The Best Business Concept

The focus of this chapter is how to design a business around a specific marketplace opportunity. When you see a marketplace opportunity, whether it involves starting a new business, refocusing your existing business, or expanding into a new area, you have to design an effective method of taking advantage of that opportunity. This is what I call your *business concept*. In general, every business concept should (1) maintain a strong customer orientation; (2) allow for the maximum flow of information; (3) be flexible enough to change as customers, technologies, and economic conditions change; and (4) be a business that you love.

Wait a minute, you may protest, "I've found a good marketplace opportunity. And I know what business concept to use. What I need to do now is stop philosophizing and start building the concept." If this is what you're thinking, you're wrong. Regardless of what you may believe, you are not ready to begin.

FINAL DECISIONS MEAN NO MORE INFORMATION

To better understand why, consider how most would-be businesspeople go about building a business. What typically happens is that, having seen a marketplace opportunity, the individuals quickly identify a business concept and run with it. They never question whether it is the best one. They never evaluate any other options. Rather, they become focused on starting **that** particular business, no matter what.

Never, perhaps, is too strong a word but I use it to emphasize how little thought and research can go into deciding on a business concept. And worse, once the decision is made, it usually becomes final. **No path to failure is more direct than a "final" decision because *final* means no more information.** Yes, decisions have to be made. Yes, you have to move ahead with a total focus on the goal. But the goal is the process, and every decision is simply another step in the process. Most often businesses fail not because of the lack of a viable opportunity but because those responsible respond to the opportunity like someone wearing blinders. For a horse in a race, perhaps, blinders have a value but not for a person in business. With blinders, you become locked into the business concept that first occurs to you and blocked from any new information that tells you not to go ahead or to go ahead in a different direction. When you're wearing blinders you have no choice. You can't go in the best direction. You can go only in the direction that's in front of you.

In many cases, businesspeople put on the blinders almost as a defense. They think of it as a way to maintain their determination, energy, and dedication. They are afraid of any distraction. They are afraid of indecision. They are afraid of learning anything that may cause them to doubt themselves or their plans. In the corporate world, Raymond Smith, chairman of Bell Atlantic, comments:[1]

---

[1]Raymond W. Smith, "Business as War Game: A Report from the Battlefront," *Fortune* (September 30, 1996), pp. 190–193.

Most successful executives are temperamentally unsuited to second-guessing their own decisions; once they set out on a certain path, they become emotionally invested in their own assumptions and come to believe that further analysis breeds waffling and indecision.

To counteract this tendency, Bell Atlantic has instituted what it calls a *manage the business process*, which "prompts managers to question . . . underlying assumptions." Smith says,

organizations must learn to analyze, adjust, even change direction in mid-flight, without losing the sense of purpose and action required in the competitive world.

In instituting this policy, Smith and Bell Atlantic are right on target. **Rather than fearing more information, decision makers should really be afraid of focusing their determination, energy, and dedication in the wrong direction.** This is a terrible waste. What you need to do is remove your blinders and devote your determination, energy, and dedication to the rhythm of business and follow it wherever it leads. This means having an awareness of everything going on around you, so that you can gather, process, and connect all the information you need. This means having the flexibility to change a business concept as often as necessary until you truly satisfy your customers. And this means, even after you've gotten everything right, maintaining that same level of vigilance and flexibility, because your customers' wants and needs change over time.

DESIGNING A CONCEPT WITH RHYTHM

One easy way to begin building a business concept around your customers is through your company's mission statement. Make it clear that your primary goal is to satisfy your customers. The more your company immerses itself in this philosophy, the more that philosophy becomes a reality and the more successful your business will be. Second, organize your company using a flatter, more horizontal structure. Some executives believe that the more levels they have in their company's organizational structure, the more successful they are. However, the reality is the more levels that exist between you and your customers, employees, suppliers, and investors, the more out of touch you are. Your flow of information becomes distorted; and once your flow of information is distorted, you no longer can feel the rhythm of your business. You are unable to tell how well or how poorly you are satisfying your customers and, worse, your ability to put your finger on what's right or wrong is weakened. **No matter how large your company grows, it is absolutely essential that you maintain direct contact with your key information sources— your customers, your suppliers, your employees, and your investors.** Third, emphasize flexibility throughout your company. We've talked about how you have to be prepared to change based on feedback from your customers. Change is essential to business, and the ability to change has to be a part of your business's culture, which leads us to our fourth point. Your company should engage in only those activities in which it has a key skill, or what today is called a *core competence*. Structuring your business around its core competencies and entering into alliances with other companies for all other needs is a low-cost concept that allows for great flexibility and, most important, allows you to do what you love—and what you love is what you do best.

VIRTUAL DANCING

When your business engages in only those activities in which it has special skills or knowledge and works with other businesses for whatever else it needs, a "network" organization, often referred to as a *virtual corporation*, is created. Essentially, virtual corporations are individual entities that rely on other companies to perform key business activities on a relationship basis. What often happens is a group of companies unite to exploit a specific marketplace opportunity and usually separate once the opportunity is satisfied. By linking together, each business focuses on what it does best, allowing the resulting virtual corporation to provide a "best of everything" strategy—the best marketing, manufacturing and distribution, and so on.[2]

This network of aligned businesses requires each member company to (1) recognize its interdependence, (2) be willing to share information, (3) cooperate with each other, and (4) customize its product or service to maintain its position within the network. Consequently, the resulting virtual corporation appears less as a traditional stand-alone business and more as an ever-changing group of businesses with mutually enhancing core competencies, all focused on satisfying the individual customer's changing wants and needs.

As you'd expect, virtual corporations demand a complex set of entrepreneurial skills and abilities—building relationships, negotiating win-win deals, finding the "right" partners with compatible goals and values, and providing the temporary organization with the appropriate balance of freedom and control. The spirit of the relationships among networked members needs to be captured in the concept of "codestiny," with each member's fate shared with that of the others.

Let's take a look at how some businesses use virtual corporations to capitalize on marketplace opportunities. Paul Farrow, for example, wanted more than his own company. He wanted to be the company all by himself. With Walden Paddlers he laid the groundwork for the ultimate virtual corporation: one employee, a network of suppliers and retailers, and—best of all—real growth potential:[3]

> Walden Paddlers has designed, produced, and marketed a technically sophisticated kayak fashioned from recycled plastic, one that significantly undercuts its competition on price and outmaneuvers it in performance. Moreover, Farrow has done all that

---

[2]W. H. Davidow and M. S. Malone, *The Virtual Corporation* (New York: Harper-Business, 1992).
[3]Edward O. Welles, "Virtual Realities," *Inc.* (August 1993), pp. 50–58.

with just one employee—himself. He deliberately set out to weave a web of strategic partnerships around Walden to avoid building a costly, cumbersome, slow-footed organization. Farrow sought, instead, to leverage as much as possible the skills of creative outsiders and dedicated specialists like himself to share risks, reduce development time, and save money, while hitting a broad slice of the market as fast as he could.

On a practical level, he estimated that building a single organization that would design, manufacture, and market kayaks would cost in excess of $1 million—money he most assuredly lacked. Farrow figured that with his plan, his total investment, to get from idea to market, would be in the "low six figures," or roughly one-tenth what he might have spent otherwise. But for all that to come together, he knew he had to forge the right strategic alliances and make what he now acknowledges was a "leap of faith."

Walden Paddlers, for all its low-tech aura, is what is known in today's fast-paced economy as a "virtual corporation," a company that outsources just about everything in the pursuit of eternal flexibility, low overhead, and the leading edge.

Or, consider Ruth Owades. When she first crafted close partnerships with suppliers in her industry, she hadn't even started her company: [4]

> Calyx & Corolla, which she founded in 1988, is a catalog operation and sells flowers and plants. Orders are processed at the Calyx office in San Francisco, and the flowers are shipped directly from growers to customers via overnight delivery. But whereas few partnerships were key to the success of Owades' first business (Gardener's Eden, which she sold to Williams-Sonoma in 1982 for $1 million), her second venture is *completely dependent* on alliances with the growers and the shipper.
>
> Because of its alliances, Calyx & Corolla has moved past the start-up stage sooner than most new companies do. In 1992 the company exceeded its goal of breaking even, posting profits greater than 5% on sales of $10 million.
>
> She is debating whether to take the company public or seek additional private financing or other relationships to obtain the

---

[4]Leslie Brokaw, "Twenty-Eight Steps to a Strategic Alliance," *Inc.* (April 1993), pp. 96–104.

cash to keep Calyx growing. While acknowledging that it remains a challenge to get potential new customers to catch on to the idea, Owades is still confident, she says, that Calyx & Corolla can eventually be a $100 million business. Her partners, so far, concur.

Both Paul Farrow and Ruth Owades have built successful businesses in this new technology- and information-intensive environment. They have put up with more than the usual fuzziness in their organizational charts in exchange for quick growth and agile businesses that draw heavily on outside relationships and technology to guide their products from their dreams to the marketplace. And, of course, when designing your business concept, as Adrian Slywotzky says in *Value Migration*, your primary consideration is not what's best for you, but what's best for your customers:[5]

> The most important question to ask when creating a business design is "what's important to the customer?" Small companies tend to ask that question more easily than do large companies, which often focus first on what's good for their own economies. The reason large companies do that is because they usually have a vested interest in a large asset base and a well-established way of doing business. They often work to protect those things, even if it means ignoring the fact that their customers have changed in a fundamental way. The less asset-intensive your business design, the more you're able to change when your customers change. For example, there's no need to lock yourself into a large investment that may become obsolete in a few years. That's true whether you're talking about computer systems or warehouses.

BUILDING YOUR CONCEPT AROUND YOUR VISION

Whether you're starting a business or launching a new product or service, no discussion of how to design a business around a marketplace opportunity would be complete without talking

[5]Adrian J. Slywotzky, *Value Migration* (Boston: Harvard Business School Press, 1996).

about vision. Regardless of how vague or incomplete your business idea is, it probably consists of two aspects: some product or service you want to sell and some means of delivering it, like theater tickets sold at booths in malls. This idea, again regardless of how vague, is the basis of what we can call your vision—your goal of what you want to accomplish. And building a business around that goal is how you make your vision a reality. Consider Ruth Owades's vision for Calyx & Corolla:[6]

> The idea of a flower catalog stuck because the concept made sense. Most flowers are cut, transported to a distributor, transported to a retailer, and transported yet again to a customer—taking anywhere from 6 to 10 days on average to go from soil to vase.
>
> As Owades envisioned it, flowers chosen from a catalog, in which customers could see exactly what they were buying, would be cut one day and reach the recipient the next.
>
> Not only would the process put customers more in command of their orders, but flowers would be more vibrant and longer lasting. By her calculations it could be done at prices comparable with those for ordering flowers via FTD.

At the time Ruth had this vision for her company she was not able to see exactly how her business could get the job done. All she had in her vision were some key features: customers using catalogs to order cut flowers and plants and having them delivered wherever her customers wanted on the very next day. Here's how Ruth describes it:[7]

> I envisioned a table with three legs, and Calyx & Corolla was only one of them. The second was the best flower growers available, and the third was Federal Express, the number one air carrier.

[6]Brokaw, 1993, p. 98.
[7]David Wylie, "Calyx & Corolla," Harvard Business School, Case No. 9-592-035 rev. 1/9/95, p. 6.

Now all Ruth had to do was figure out how to put together all the parts of her vision and make it a reality.

At this point, what Ruth Owades or any businessperson needs is information. In Ruth Owades's case, she needed to know the inner workings of the flower and mail-order businesses to see how best she could combine them. She had to go to trade shows, read mail-order catalogs, talk to people in the industry, talk to customers, and the like. In short, she had to do everything she could to gather, process, and connect as much information as possible. She had to find growers to sell the flowers, negotiate with FedEx to deliver the flowers, find an artist to put together the catalog, and so on. So, day by day, breakthrough by breakthrough, connection by connection, slowly, lovingly, and with a lot of energy and effort, she put together all the legs of the "table" and made her own vision a reality.

VISION SHAPES REALITY, REALITY SHAPES VISION

Perhaps, more accurately, we could say putting together all the "legs" of her business was a matter of her vision and reality meeting. She had her initial vision of Calyx & Corolla, but as she tried to bring that vision into reality, her vision changed due to the practicalities of customers, money, circumstances, time, technology, and so forth. In other words, her vision shaped reality and reality shaped her vision. Maybe, in her vision, she pictured a 32-page catalog with lots of photographs but in reality she could afford only a 16-page catalog; and instead of photographs, she discovered a fantastic and inexpensive illustrator whom she felt would give her catalog the unique look she wanted. Thus, in the meeting of her vision and reality, both changed and both grew.

Does this mean Ruth Owades's original vision was wrong or that Ruth Owades had a poor vision of her business? No. It means that most people have an incomplete understanding of what vision is. Vision is not a perfect picture of the future. Just as no one can write a perfect business plan, no one has a perfect vision of the future. Vision is an idea combined with an instinctive understanding for the rhythm of business. A true visionary always is walking that fine line between sticking with an idea and having the flexibility to change the idea when reality requires it. The misunderstanding about vision occurs because successful businesspeople are noticed by their peers, the business press, and academic analysts **after** they already have achieved some measure of success, after they've managed to build a successful business. To these observers, successful businesspeople seem to have a very clear vision. How could they arrive at their goal unless they always had it in their sights?

But that is not how business success occurs. Think back to our Drucker and Kahn quotes. Businesses do not succeed in the way they begin. Why? Because business success is not a straight line. Business is a process, a rhythm. And as you dance to that rhythm, as you go through the steps of planning, preparing, interacting, analyzing and refining, your business develops. You start with your vision, no matter how vague it is, Then, as you attempt to bring that vision into reality, through every step of the rhythm, your vision grows, changes. What you can do, you do. What information you need, you get. What has to change, you change. What has to be learned, you learn. You start small. You ask. You experiment. You test. You work hard. Gradually your vision and reality merge and become your business.

Look at the many transformations David Woo's vision went through:[8]

> Back in 1988 Woo and his two partners—all graduate students at the University of California—were getting ready to shut down a computer consulting firm they had founded, having chewed through their $25,000 in financing.
>
> Then came the call: a customer had an urgent question about his computers. Nobody was in the office, but the voice-mail system beeped Woo. When he returned the call immediately from

[8]Stephen D. Solomon, "The Best (Way)laid Plans," *Inc. 500* (1996), p. 69. Excerpted with permission from *Inc.* magazine 1996. Copyright 1996 by Goldhirsh Group. Inc., 38 Commercial Wharf, Boston, MA 02110.

the road, the customer expressed amazement. What was this system that could not only record messages but also tug at Woo's shirtsleeve many miles away? Could Woo install one for him, too?

In the split second it took Woo to respond, a new business formed in his mind. He quickly tracked down the manufacturer of the voice-mail system. "We called and said we had a customer for them," he says. Woo also proposed that he and his partners become a dealer for the manufacturer in southern and central California.

For Woo, the chief executive, the transformation from consulting company to voice-mail seller and installer turned out to be only the first of several he would engineer. Two years later the company's sales tumbled from $800,000 to $400,000 because, Woo says, the two manufacturers he represented fell behind the competition. Automatic Answer could have signed on with other manufacturers, but the partners saw that their position would not be appreciably different: their success would still depend too much on third parties. "We weren't comfortable with that," Woo says.

The solution: design voice-mail systems of their own. As the three cofounders wrote the programs, they piled on debt. One of them, Simak Emadi, borrowed $200,000 on a collection of personal credit cards. "It was pretty bleak," says Woo. The turning point: the company found equipment manufacturers that would buy the systems and then sell them under their own names.

But Automatic Answer wasn't through with its metamorphosis. In late 1995 Woo decided to diversify by selling the company's voice-mail system under its own brand name, Amanda. Sales of Amanda represented 25% of the company's $8.8 million in revenues in 1995, and that figure will soar to about 50% in 1997.

Not that Woo likes to plan that far ahead.

TIM DEMELLO'S VISION MEETS REALITY

Even if your business does not change that dramatically or quickly, your business and your vision will change. Here is another example from Tim DeMello as he went through his business building process with his company, Streamline. Early on, he described his vision thus:

Imagine that it has been a long hard week and you return to your house and waiting for you in your Streamline pantry is your week's worth of groceries, your dry cleaning, the pictures from your daughter's birthday and the new video you have been wanting to watch. Tonight, you can decompress watching the video, knowing that in the morning you can sleep in because you don't have to run around to a dozen different stores like you used to do every Saturday morning.

Now, as it happens, this early description of Tim's business still is generally accurate but, of course, missing are the specifics of how Tim was going to accomplish his goal. How did Tim arrive at these specifics? If we look at Tim's building business process, we see that, although the process Tim uses is very systematic and well thought out, the business itself grows, develops, and changes in a very natural way as his vision meets reality.

From the beginning Tim's vision was of a company that provided a large array of products and services, yet Tim felt that the best way to start was small, offering one specific home service. This would keep his costs low and allow him to begin designing his business according to what he learned from his own research and customer feedback. Tim's initial understanding of his marketplace opportunity led him to believe that his customers had the following profile:

> The company's primary target customers live in owner-occupied houses, consisting of dual-wage or time-starved adults in the 30 to 50 age group, who earn $50,000 or more per year, and more than likely have children and a pet.

This type of customer was targeted because of the inherent needs associated with owning a home, the purchasing power of this market segment, and the time constraints placed on these individuals as they tried to balance the demands of career and families.

As discussed in Chapter 5, Tim began his customer testing process by offering one service to approximately 50 households. After doing a lot of research on various home-delivery service options, Tim decided to start by offering a home-delivery dry cleaning service. He selected dry cleaning because the business:

- Was easy to enter,
- Required no inventory,
- Had relatively high operating margins,
- Was a good stand-alone product,
- Fit the customer demographic profile,
- Should produce $600–700 in annualized revenue per household.

Having decided on dry cleaning, Tim next had to determine how he would provide the service. Tim looked at the two main activities in the business, pick-up and delivery and the actual cleaning operation; and he considered several alternatives for each. For example, he could buy a van, have it outfitted as needed, including painting it with his company logo, or he could lease a vehicle and not paint it, or he could simply use his or one of his soon to be hired employees' cars. With respect to the actual cleaning, Tim considered buying a dry cleaning business, simply using a variety of local cleaners, or negotiating a special deal with one or more local cleaners in return for all of the cleaning business. In the end, Tim decided to purchase a van and negotiate a special arrangement (i.e., a strategic alliance) with the owners of two dry cleaning businesses, one for shirts and one for everything else.

Tim figured that having the van with his company's name on it would be important because the customers actually would "see" the van and interact with the driver. However, he reasoned that, as long as he maintained the highest dry cleaning standards, it wouldn't matter to his customers whether he owned the cleaning operation. When Tim first envisioned Streamline he "saw" a company delivery van going through the neighborhoods. However, when he first started the company he wasn't sure what would be in the van and he wasn't sure how it would get into the van, but he always knew there had to be a van. Therefore, it was easy for Tim to decide to invest in the van and use an outside service for the dry cleaning. At the moment, he wasn't even sure whether dry cleaning would wind up in his final mix of products and services.

Although his decisions at this early time in his business building process appear simple enough, Tim carefully thought through all facets of each decision. I should point out, however, that Tim was not expecting to make money providing his service to only 50 customers. Rather, he expected to lose money on every transaction. But it didn't matter. For the moment, making money was not what he was trying to do. He was focused on gathering information about his customers as well as developing the business concept that would most effectively satisfy those customers.

Tim also used a number of different approaches to acquire the desired 50 test customers. In addition to using his own family, Tim recruited friends and neighbors as well as people who had heard about the home delivery service and wanted to try it. Throughout the test period, Tim had numerous conversations with his customers to find out how his service was doing and to identify other products and services they would be interested in.

From a business concept standpoint, one of the key observations Tim made during his first cycle of customer interaction was the desirability of freeing the customer from being home when the dry cleaning van picked up or delivered. It was clear that his customers wanted more freedom from waiting for the drivers and his drivers wanted more freedom in their timing of the pickup and deliveries. But the question was how to arrange that freedom. In thinking this problem through, Tim came up with the idea of a compact, efficient, and secure receptacle, consisting of separate compartments for frozen, refrigerated, and dry goods that could be installed easily in a home (or garage). Tim worked with his father to design a prototype service receptacle (see Figure 6–1) and installed it in his garage so he could use it during his second cycle of customer interaction. (By customer interaction cycle 5, Tim had entered into a strategic alliance with GE to redesign and supply the service receptacle.) Once he had the receptacle installed, the homeowner would not have to be present to interact with the driver. The information Tim gathered from cycle 1 also led him to conclude that, to really

Streamline Inc.
Service Receptacle
Figure 6–1

provide value to the customer, he had to position his business as a scheduled delivery service to the home (providing a custom-ized mix of products and services) rather than as an on-demand (grocery) delivery to the customer, as was being tried by some new supermarket delivery services.

Based on the input received during cycle 1, Tim decided that, during cycle 2, he should offer multiple products and ser-vices to a single customer and, further, that his family would be that customer. Several kinks still had to be worked through before he tried the multiple services on other customers, and he felt he could best analyze whatever changes were needed if he and his family were directly involved. Accordingly, Tim added groceries, health and beauty aids, video rentals, and beer, wine, and spirits to the goods he would deliver. Also, Tim continued to serve his original cycle 1 dry cleaning customers, even though he had moved on to cycle 2. Besides, his customers valued the service so much they didn't want him to stop.

As in cycle 1, Tim faced a number of decisions about how he should put together his business to provide his customers (his own family) what they wanted. For example, he had to decide how they would order what they wanted (by telephone, fax, or computer), where he would do the consolidation (rent a resource center or use someone else's facility), where and how he would source the products (did he have to "own" the inven-tory or just have access to it), and how much he should charge.

Because this was a test, Tim made sure to try a number of different methods of carrying out each of the company's key activities. And his focus was always on learning which method was the most effective at satisfying his customers' desires. In addition, Tim made use of a PC database to more easily gather and process all pertinent customer information.

After two months of cycle 2 testing, Tim again paused to assess what he had learned and refine his understanding of his customers and how best to satisfy their wants and needs. For example, Tim learned (1) the service receptacle needed to be redesigned to take up less space, (2) it was possible to include food and nonfood grocery items as part of the service, and (3) once the system had been set up, it would be easy to work with the customer to identify additional products and services that could be included in the delivery service. Tim also learned that his current system of order entry and order fulfillment needed improvement. Then, based on this information, Tim made what he felt were the appropriate adjustments and redesigned his business concept for cycle 3.

As in the two previous customer interaction cycles, Tim clearly identified specific learning objectives for cycle 3. Tim wanted to evaluate alternate pricing structures and identify and evaluate alternative sourcing strategies for his key products and services. This information, Tim felt, would help him determine which products and services Streamline should focus on, either by development from within or by acquisition of suppliers and which ones should be carried out through a partnership (alliance). In addition, Tim wanted to refine and test the systems, personnel, facility, and equipment requirements needed to service a number of customer households with a customized mix of products and services. Thus, for cycle 3, he tested a multitude of product and services for six customers.

While cycle 3 went well, at the end of the test cycle, Tim had to decide whether he had sufficient understanding to ramp up to full (resource center) operation or to carry out another test cycle. Someone once said that genius is the "infinite capacity of taking pains." It takes a lot of work to get things right, and in a business, even though you're always eager to move ahead, it's important to only move ahead when you're ready; so, as discussed in Chapter 5, Tim decided to take more pains and carry out a fourth cycle of testing.

RHYTHM/TIMING/FEELING

What criterion did Tim use as the basis for this decision? Tim wanted to see in his data what he describes as the "clearly positive feedback from customers that he was satisfying their desires," but that is, perhaps, a dry way of stating it. In reality, Tim was looking for his "customer's vote." He was looking for a clear indication that his customers wanted his product or service, and this type of customer response has to jump out at you. In your cash register receipts, database, spreadsheet, phone call logs, or whatever method you use to track your sales, you need to see something that says you've got it or, at least, you're well on your way to getting it. How big a jump should that be? That's where your instinct, your feeling, your rhythm has to come in. Those with natural-born rhythm will see it immediately and know it. Those with less developed rhythm might hesitate and wait a little too long or not long enough. However, although timing is extremely important, you can only use the best rhythm/timing/feeling you have at the moment you need to make the decision. You can't wait until your timing is better or until you think your timing is perfect. No one's timing is perfect. You have to start your business, and if you follow the rhythm of business, you'll understand that, even if you're a little bit off, business consists of repeated customer interaction cycles; and as long as you follow these cycles, every cycle will move you closer to providing your customers with exactly what they want and need.

Consequently, using his own rhythm/timing/feeling, Tim decided that he wasn't comfortable enough with the response of his customers in cycle 3. So he designed customer interaction cycle 4. It was a large-scale market ramp to approximately 100 customer households using a modified mix of products and services. This fourth cycle allowed Tim to gather more specific information about how to get target households to sign on as customers as well as to continue refining the order generation and fulfillment processes so critical to the success of his business.

In addition to these tests, Tim used the period to study the operating methods of several companies recognized as having world-class levels of customer satisfaction. Included in this evaluation were FedEx, L.L. Bean, and Jordan's Furniture. These companies had received recognition in the business press as being the "best in the world" in areas that Tim knew were important to Streamline's success. Tim wanted to understand exactly how these companies did things so he could adopt a similar approach in his design of Streamline's operations.

At the end of cycle 4, Tim felt he had reached the level of understanding required for Streamline to move ahead to cycle 5 and open its first (prototype) Customer Resource Center. He felt that he had a strong enough response from his customers, based on a significant and sustained increase in weekly household sales, to introduce his home delivery services on a wide scale to towns within a 15-mile radius and handle up to 2,000 customer households.

Thus, we can see how carefully Tim grew his company around his market opportunity. He started with his vision and, cycle by cycle, developed it, shaped it, changed it, and the realities of the marketplace developed, shaped, and changed his vision until he had a functioning business.

KEY POINTS IN CHAPTER 6

• Every business concept should (1) maintain a strong customer orientation; (2) allow for the maximum flow of information; (3) be flexible enough to change as customers, technologies, and economic conditions change; and (4) be a business that you love.

• No path to failure is more direct than a "final" decision because *final* means no more information.

• Rather than fearing more information, decision makers should really be afraid of focusing their determination, energy, and dedication in the wrong direction.

• Make it clear that your primary goal is to satisfy your customers.

• Organize your company using a flatter, more horizontal structure. The more levels between you and your customers, employees, suppliers, and investors, the more out of touch you are.

• Your company should engage in only those activities in which it has a key skill, or what today is called a *core competence*. Structuring your business around its core competencies and entering into alliances with other companies for all other needs is a concept that allows for great flexibility, and most important, allows you to do what you love, because what you love is what you do best.

• A network of aligned businesses requires each member company to (1) recognize its interdependence, (2) be willing to share information, (3) cooperate with each other, and (4) customize its product or service to maintain its position within the network.

• Regardless of how vague or incomplete your business idea is, it probably consists of two aspects: some product or service you want to sell and some means of delivering it, like theater tickets sold at booths in malls. This idea, again regardless of how vague, is the basis of what we can call your vision—your goal of what you want to accomplish.

• Vision is not a perfect picture of the future. Just as no one can write a perfect business plan, no one has a perfect vision of the future. Vision is an idea combined with an instinctive understanding for the rhythm of business. A true visionary always is walking that fine line between sticking with an idea and having the flexibility to change the idea when reality requires it.

• You start with your vision, no matter how vague it is; then, as you attempt to bring that vision into reality, through every step of the rhythm, your vision grows, changes, and develops and your business grows, changes, and develops.

• No one's timing is perfect. You have to start your business; and if you follow the rhythm of business, you'll understand that even if you're a little bit off, business consists of repeated customer interaction cycles. As long as you follow those cycles, every cycle will move you closer to providing your customers with exactly what they want and need.

Happiness is a positive cash flow.

...FRED ADLER

7

Raising Money and Motivating People

The rhythm of business requires discovering who your customers are, finding out what those customers' want and need, developing a business concept to satisfy those wants and needs, **and** assembling the resources required to make that business concept happen. In addition, as you work your way toward the ideal business, customer interaction cycle after customer interaction cycle, you need to assemble and reassemble your resources to accommodate any changes. This task is not small or easy. "Assembling the resources" requires a great deal of time, skill, and money. And, depending on the size of your business, both at startup and as it grows, the task of assembling resources can seem overwhelming.

So how do you do it? How do you put together the resources you need? Clearly, you must first identify the resources; and I'm sure, if you were to sit down and write out a list—even without doing much research—you'd quickly fill up a few pages. However, for our purposes, I'm going to concentrate on the two major resources needed to start and grow any business: money and people. As shown in Figure 7–1, **if you are going to build and run a successful business, you must be able to motivate the money and people resources around your vision.**

EVERY DECISION HAS A FINANCIAL IMPACT

Many times, when people talk about being successful in business, they say they would like to be successful so they can make money, a lot of money. What's really surprising is that the majority of these people actually know very little about money. I'm not talking about how to spend money, we all know how to do that. Rather, I'm talking about something much more important—the role money plays in building a successful business. And that's unfortunate because, **if you want to be successful in business, you must understand money.** Money is the lifeblood of business. In Chapter 3, I said that information permeates every aspect of the rhythm of business. Well, money does, too.

Of course, you need not be an accountant or a CPA to understand the role of money. But, you do need to understand the financial impact of the thousands of decisions and actions required to build and run a business. Simply saying that your accountant does that misses the point. Sure, an accountant can help work through money matters, but his or her advice lacks some very important elements—it's not the accountant's business and it's not the accountant's money, nor is that person's emotional, intellectual, and financial well-being at risk. It's yours. Quite frankly, I emphasize this point because of what I learned to my dismay in the software business. I am still astonished at the lack of interest so many businesspeople have in understanding how to take control of their financial decisions. You may not want to learn this, but you have to. Relying on financial advisors, no matter how expert, is not good enough. **Unless you understand the financial impact of your business decisions, you will not feel the rhythm of business and you will not be successful in business.**

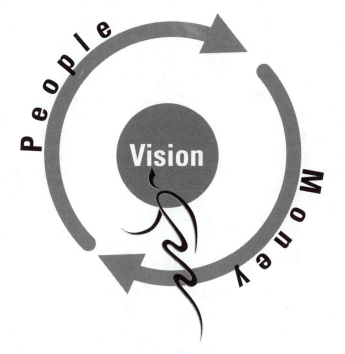

Motivating Key Resources
Figure 7–1

FINDING THE LOWEST COST CONCEPT

What do you need to know about money? As I mentioned, an important aspect of the rhythm of business is carrying out a series of low-cost, fast-paced customer interaction cycles aimed at increasing your understanding of your customers and the business concept best able to satisfy them. During Step 1, the planning phase, you want to identify and evaluate various alternative business concepts and choose the specific concept you think is best for that cycle. Consequently, one of the first things you want to discover is which of the many possible business concepts truly costs the least. Of course, the one that costs the least is not necessarily the one you will eventually choose, because other factors may override cost. But you have to know which costs the least, and you need to accurately estimate your company's revenues and expenses for whichever business concept you do use.

THE CASH FLOW STATEMENT

In addition to determining how much money you need, you also have to figure out when you will need the money and where you're going to get it. Whether you're inside a large existing company and you get your money from the chief financial officer or own your own business and have to raise the money (which usually means selling equity in your business), you have to calculate how much money you need and when you will need it. This figuring, perhaps, sounds like a lot of work, and it is; but the good news is that you can use one fairly simple tool, called a *cash flow statement*. A cash flow statement shows the inflow of money into your business (or division) as well as the outflow of money. When the amount coming in (from sales) is greater than the amount going out (from expenses), you have a profitable business. When the amount of money coming in is less than the amount going out you have an unprofitable business and soon are out of business. Simple.

A cash flow statement is easy to understand, because it shows when you actually receive cash and when you actually pay out cash. Notice that I said *actually receive cash and actually pay out cash.* In many instances, a business "sells" its products or services and then waits to get paid, just as it may buy something and pay for it later on a credit card. Although you may get the product at the time you charge it, you do not actually pay out your cash until some time later, perhaps at the end of the month when you pay your bills.

MAKING ASSUMPTIONS

To prepare a cash flow statement, you have to make **specific** assumptions about your customers and whichever business concept you are evaluating. Unfortunately, as Samuel Goldwyn used to say, "It is tough to predict, especially about the future!" But you must do it. So it is necessary that you gather all the information you can to help make realistic assumptions about anticipated sales revenues and expenses. Remember, if your information isn't accurate the answers to the important "how much" and "when needed" questions will be unreliable and you may run out of money. So you must make sure you gather **all** the information you can about your customers and **all** the information you can about the business concept you are deciding to use. Different concepts—whether you are developing a retail store, a warehouse outlet, or a mail-order business—will mean different costs. So, when you are deciding which concept to use, you have to consider not only whether the method is best for your customers and whether it is a business you will love but how much it costs.

In the next chapter, we discuss the details that go into starting and running a business. However, it is important to stress that one of the most common mistakes in preparing a cash flow statement is leaving out a "detail," like forgetting the cost for an advertising campaign and suddenly finding yourself facing an "unexpected" $5,000 expense. This is why starting and running a business in an area you know is very helpful. You are familiar with most of the details and less likely to get caught by unexpected expenses. But we'll get to details in the next chapter. For now, as shown in Figure 7–2, understand that to prepare an accurate cash flow statement you must become comfortable making critical assumptions about your business, and to do that, you need to gather accurate information.

Ideally, if you are just starting a new business, you should do a cash flow on a daily basis. After all, when you are starting, a month or even a week is a long time, because in many instances, you are concerned about having enough cash to get through the day. Practically speaking, for most new businesses, a month-by-month cash flow should give you a good understanding of your financing needs.

How many months into the future should you forecast? Obviously, the further out into the future you go, the more unreliable your assumptions will be. In many instances, it's hard to anticipate what is going to happen tomorrow or next week, never mind 36 to 60 months from now. To be honest, in a business you are just starting, you simply don't know enough about your customers and their changing wants and needs and how your business will change to make accurate assumptions that far into the future. Consequently, I suggest that you tie your cash flow statement to the length of time you plan for each customer interaction cycle. If you anticipate that your next customer interaction cycle will last nine months, then your cash flow statement should run only nine months. If you want to prepare a cash flow statement that looks further out into the future, you certainly can do that. However, you must understand that many of the assumptions you use will change as a result of what you learn during each cycle. And, once your assumptions change, your cash flow statement changes and you will get different answers to the critical "how much" and "when needed" questions.

I should point out here that, today, the conventional practice for raising money is that bankers and investors expect you to prepare a cash flow statement that looks three to five years into

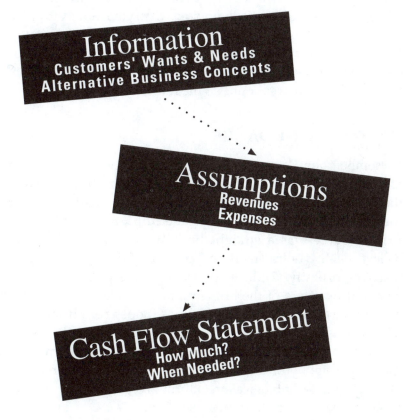

Making Assumptions

Figure 7–2

the future. And, as is the common practice, you are expected to do the first year by month, the second year by quarter, and the third, fourth, and fifth years by year. However, based on everything we've discussed, it is obvious that your ability to make correct assumptions diminishes greatly the further out you go. You simply don't know your customers, or the business environment, or your own business concept well enough to make realistic assumptions that far out into the future.

IT'S NOT A LINE DANCE

Remember our Peter Drucker and Leo Kahn quotes. I keep reminding you of them because they point out the fatal flaw in the conventional wisdom. **The conventional wisdom is completely linear. It assumes bumps and blips, but it still sees the road to success as a straight line.** The conventional wisdom believes (1) if you're smart and come up with a good marketplace opportunity, (2) develop your business plan, (3) convince potential investors of the brilliance of your plan, (4) gather the resources to make that plan a reality, (5) open for business, and (6) you do a good job with items 1–5, then you will reap the profits from your business. Again, conventional wisdom allows for the possibility of unseen circumstances, such as a recession or competing technological breakthroughs, but it still insists that a linear process leads to success. See Figure 7–3.

Nothing could be further from the truth! Business follows a rhythm, a rhythm that includes continual changes. **And as Peter Drucker and Leo Kahn point out, the business described in your carefully written business plan is rarely the successful business that develops. Natural-born business people instinctively recognize this, and although they may go through the conventional strategies of writing a business plan, intuitively, they are more focused on the rhythm than the plan and always are ready to move with the beat. They always are ready to dance.**

Businesspeople without that instinctive sense are confused and frustrated when their business doesn't turn out as expected.

Start

The Conventional Wisdom
Figure 7–3

They think they've failed. They think fate has played a dirty trick on them. Maybe if they're quick enough and flexible enough, like Woo, they blindly shift and twist their way to success and then brag to their friends that they knew what they were doing all along. But, you don't have to tell tales or think you've failed. You have to follow the rhythm of business.

My view is you always have to be ready to change your product or service and your business concept, and the old and oft recommended cash flow methods tend to prevent flexibility and keep you wedded to your initial three- to five-year plan. This happens because, once those written estimates are in the hands of your backers (investors and bankers), any deviation from them becomes a danger sign that your business is failing rather than a vital sign that your business needs to change. Who wants to reveal to his or her backers that a "mistake" was made? But, again, no one can devise a perfect business plan. "Mistakes" are inevitable. The important point is **not** to have a business but a process, a process that can correct mistakes and thereby hone in on what your customers really want and need.

You might wonder what happens if the deviations in your estimates are positive rather than negative. Well, as surprising as it may seem, it's just as easy to run into trouble if you are doing too much business as too little. I know it's hard to believe that more business can actually be bad, but it can. For example, if you have not correctly identified how much cash you need to finance your increased accounts receivable (money owed to you by your customers) or to finance increased inventory (money you owe to your suppliers) or money needed to hire additional employees, even with increases in sales, you can run out of money and your business will fail. I realize that the problems brought about by too much business may seem better than the problems brought about by too little business, but in both cases, it is a serious situation because you have insufficient cash to continue. Consequently, I feel you are much better off to link your cash flow statements to your customer interaction cycles.

However, as discussed in Chapter 2, because it is difficult to tell exactly how long a customer interaction cycle will last and you never want to run out of money, you should allow yourself a couple of months' leeway. For example, if you believe that the next interaction cycle will last 9 months, you should run the cash flow for 11 months, just in case.

This means explaining to potential lenders and investors or chief financial officers (CFOs) that your cash flow statement is tied directly to your customer interaction cycles. That, based on your increased understanding of your customers and your business concept, you will prepare a new cash flow statement for each subsequent customer interaction cycle. You also have to explain that you are doing it this way because it gives you a much better ability to answer the "how much money" and "when needed" questions than the normal five-year cash flow statement. Convincing them may take a little effort, but you need to do it. It is in your and their best interest.

THE CASH FLOW TANGO

To better understand how a cash flow statement works, let me walk you through a simple example, using Figure 7–4. In this example, the cash flow statement concerns a business you are starting, and your first customer interaction cycle begins in January and lasts approximately 9 months. Therefore, based on what we just discussed, the cash flow statement should run from January through November. This way it covers the 9 months you believe your customer interaction cycle will last plus 2 additional months for a total of 11 months.

When creating a cash flow, the first thing you should do is write down all of the assumptions you made to prepare the statement. By doing this you can look back at your assumptions and understand what you were thinking at the time the cash flow was prepared. Remember, you will not be able to make accurate assumptions if you do not have accurate information. In our example, we have made the following assumptions:

	Jan	Feb	March	April	May	June	July	Aug	Sept	Oct	Nov
Operating Cash Inflows											
Cash Sales	$10,000	$14,000	$16,000	$18,000	$21,000	$24,000	$27,000	$33,000	$39,000	$48,000	$57,000
Total Operating Cash Inflows	10,000	14,000	16,000	18,000	21,000	24,000	27,000	33,000	39,000	48,000	57,000
Operating Cash Outflows											
Purchases	5,000	7,000	8,000	9,000	10,500	12,000	13,500	16,500	19,500	24,000	28,500
Payroll	4,500	4,500	5,500	5,500	6,500	6,500	7,500	7,500	7,500	8,500	8,500
Other Operating Expenses	5,500	6,000	7,000	7,000	7,500	8,000	8,500	8,500	8,500	8,500	8,500
Total Operating Cash Outflows	15,000	17,500	20,500	21,500	24,500	26,500	29,500	32,500	35,500	41,000	45,500
Net Operating Cash Flow	(5,000)	(3,500)	(4,500)	(3,500)	(3,500)	(2,500)	(2,500)	500	3,500	7,000	11,500
Non Operating Inflows/Outflows											
Add:											
Beginning Cash Balance	0	(5,000)	(8,500)	(13,000)	(16,500)	(20,000)	(22,500)	(25,000)	(24,500)	(21,000)	(14,000)
Money Invested (Equity)											
Money Borrowed (Debt)											
Subtract:											
Debt Repayment											
Interest Payments											
Taxes											
Total Non Operating Inflows/Outflows	0	(5,000)	(8,500)	(13,000)	(16,500)	(20,000)	(22,500)	(25,000)	(24,500)	(21,000)	(14,000)
Ending Cash Balance	($5,000)	($8,500)	($13,000)	($16,500)	($20,000)	($22,500)	($25,000)	($24,500)	($21,000)	($14,000)	($2,500)

( ) Means negative number

Cash Flow Statement
Figure 7–4

1. All sales to customers are paid in cash at the time of the sale.
2. Items purchased from suppliers must be paid for when purchased.
3. Operating expenses start at $5,500 and increase monthly until they reach $8,500 per month, at which time they remain constant.
4. There is no beginning cash balance.
5. Payroll must be paid in the month incurred.
6. Purchases are 50 percent of sales revenues.
7. The customer interaction cycle will last nine months.

The first section of the cash flow statement, Operating Cash Inflows, refers to the amount of cash coming into your business from the normal operations of the business. At this point, we focus on the operations of the company (i.e., sales to your customers) and therefore do not want to include any monies that may be invested in or loaned to the company. We do it this way to determine the true amount of cash required by the business over and above the cash generated by the company's normal business operations.

The second row, Cash Sales, shows how much of your product and service you will actually sell and be paid for each month. How do you know what your sales are going to be and when you'll get paid? That's a good question. And you need to be able to answer it, because **forecasting sales is the most important assumption you make since it directly influences most of your other assumptions**. So, let's look at how you make this determination. You may recall that I've repeatedly stated that the rhythm of business is based on understanding your customers and that this understanding comes from gathering, processing, and connecting information. Well, part of the information you gather has to deal with how much of your product or service your customers will buy and when they'll actually buy and pay for it.

Before you open your business, your information naturally is most susceptible to error. If you are starting a business in an area you know because of your own work experience or a hobby, then you have some knowledge and understanding to go on. If you have done your own market research or hired professionals to do it, then you have that additional information. If you've gone to trade shows and talked to others in similar businesses, you also have that information. But even with all these sources and any others you might use, before you open for business (and this is the case for step 1, cycle 1), any assumption you make is just that, an assumption, a guesstimate. But guesstimate or not, it has to be made. Clearly, it's best to be very careful and try to get the best information you can. After you've gone through cycle 1 and have direct market input from your customers, your assumptions on your next cash flow statement, covering your second customer interaction cycle will be more accurate. But you still need some figures to begin with, and as long as they are your best guesstimate, that has to be good enough.

IDENTIFYING YOUR CASH REQUIREMENTS

In this example, for simplicity's sake, we assumed that your customers will pay you in cash at the time of the sale. Unfortunately, it often doesn't work that way. In many instances, you will extend credit to your customers. For example, you may sell a customer a sport jacket for $150 and allow the customer to pay you 30 days later. In this case, your sale to the customer might be in April, but the receipt of the $150 in cash will not show up on the cash flow statement until you actually collect the money in May. Of course, you also may be able to buy things from your suppliers and pay for them 30 or even 60 days after you get them, but what I am trying to do here is not make an accountant out of you. I am just trying to make the concept clear.

The next row, Total Operating Cash Inflows, is the sum of the above rows, which in our example is the same as the cash sales row because we are getting paid at the time of the sale.

Now, you have to turn your attention to the money going out of your company. This section is labeled Operating Cash Outflows to remind you that it shows when the money is actually paid out, not when the obligations are incurred. Once again, you have to make assumptions. Only this time they are about when you actually have to pay for the items used by your business.

In this example, again for simplicity's sake, we have assumed that you pay for the materials purchased at the time you receive them. This is a realistic assumption, as suppliers will be reluctant to extend credit to a new business. The next row shows your payroll costs, which are assumed to be paid in the month incurred. To make this example as easy as possible, in the Other Operating Expenses row, I have grouped several separate expense categories. This row includes such things as rent and utilities, sales and marketing, and general and administrative expenses. Again, using the information about your business you collected, you need to make assumptions about the exact month in which these expenses actually will be paid. Once you've listed all of the cash outflows, your total operating cash outflows are calculated by adding all of the figures in the outflow rows.

Now that we've calculated the total monthly inflows and outflows, we simply subtract the outflows from the inflows to get the net operating cash flow. This row shows us exactly how much cash is generated or needed by your business each month. In this example, we can see that in January, the first month of actual operation, your business has a net operating cash flow of minus $5,000. This means that, under the assumptions made, your business needs to pay out $5,000 more than it took in. That is, your business requires an additional $5,000 to cover its operating obligations in the month of January.

The next section of the cash flow statement, Non Operating Inflows/Outflows, covers the monies coming into and going out of your business from other than its normal operations. As you can see, I organized these inflows and outflows into groups that you either add to or subtract from the cash you have. The first row in the "add" subgroup is Beginning Cash Balance. This row shows the cash in your business (most likely in your business checking account) at the start of each month. As you can see, I assumed that you have a $0 cash balance in your checking account at the start of January, which means that the ending cash balance for January shows a minus $5,000, reflecting the minus operating cash flow.

Where are you going to get it? Well, in addition to money flowing into your business from sales to your customers (i.e., through its normal operations), money can be loaned to or invested in your business. Therefore, I labeled the next two rows Money Invested (equity) and Money Borrowed (debt). But, as you can see, we have not shown any figures in either row, because for the moment, we are using the cash flow statement to determine the actual cash requirements of the business. We'll get to loans and investments a bit later.

I also included rows for Debt Repayment and Interest Payments. If you in fact wind up borrowing money, then at some point you have to start making payments to your lender. These rows allow you to show the repayment of the money borrowed (principal) as well as the interest you have to pay the lender for letting you borrow the money. Again, because we are assuming no money borrowed at this time, no entries are in either of these rows.

The next row, Taxes, probably requires no explanation, because we all know that taxes have to be paid. To be honest, this can get very complicated, so for our purposes I simply show one row that would cover any local, state, or federal taxes owed by your business. Most likely, your accountant will help you with this section of the cash flow. However, again keeping things simple, we show no entries under the tax row. The last row in this section, Total Non Operating Inflows/Outflows, simply is the total of the rows in this section. In our example, the total for January is $0, the same as the amount in the beginning cash balance, because you have made no entries in any other row. By quickly skipping over the blank rows, we can determine our **cash requirements**, exactly how much money we need to carry out our first customer interaction cycle, over and above the cash generated by the normal operation of the business during cycle 1.

We determine this from the Ending Cash Balance row. And as its name implies, this row shows the amount of cash your business has at the end of each month. When you look at the figures in the Ending Cash Balance row, notice that all of them are negative (in parentheses). This means that, under the set of assumptions made, you do not generate sufficient cash from the normal operations of your business to cover all the expenses required, which is typical of most new businesses. This means you need money to be invested in or loaned to the business. In fact, this is the purpose of this cash flow statement, to show you how much money you need and when you need it to carry out your customer interaction cycle.

If you look across the Ending Cash Balance row in Figure 7–4, you will notice that the negative numbers show that you need $5,000 in January, an additional $3,500 in February, $4,500 more in March, $3,500 more in April, $3,500 more in May, $2,500 more in June, and $2,500 more in July for a total of $25,000 needed overall. Also notice that, in August, the Ending Cash Balance actually improves to negative $24,500. While a $500 improvement may not seem like much, it does tell you that you had a positive operating cash flow during that month. The August figure for Net Operating Cash Flow shows a positive $500, which is why the Ending Cash Balance has improved. And it continues to improve during September, which was assumed to be the last month of this customer interaction cycle, and October and November, the two extra months we included as part of cycle 1's cash flow to be on the "safe" side. So, as you can see, this statement not only shows you how much money is needed overall for your customer interaction cycle but also when you need it on a month-by-month basis.

Given the assumptions made, this cash flow statement tells you that you need a total of $25,000 to carry out your first customer interaction cycle. If you were to go back to your entries for January and put $25,000 in the Money Invested row (previously left blank), and then run out the cash flow for the rest of the 11 months, you would now see that the Ending Cash Balance in July is $0, as shown in Figure 7–5. That is, the cash flow statement (Figure 7–4) showed that you needed $25,000 to fund the business concept under consideration and, once you include that additional money (Figure 7–5), all of the negative entries in the Ending Cash Balance row become either positive or zero balances.

However, because you have to make perhaps dozens of individual assumptions to prepare a cash flow statement, you need to realize that, if your assumptions are off (e.g., things cost more than you thought or you didn't sell as much as planned), then the $25,000 you raised would be insufficient to get you through the cycle. Therefore, to be on the safe side, you should always allow some sort of a cushion (extra cash) when you are figuring out how much money you need. The truth of the matter is that it is hard to say how much "extra" cash you should have, but make sure you allow yourself perhaps 10 to 20 percent to cover those contingencies. And they do happen.

BE CAREFUL ABOUT YOUR ASSUMPTIONS

While we're talking about your assumptions, remember, if you change any of your assumptions, you wind up changing how much money you need and when you need it. So, before borrowing money or selling part of the business, carefully review your assumptions. See if it is possible (and realistic) to change one or more of your assumptions so that you can improve your cash flow and reduce the money you need. However, be very careful when reviewing and changing assumptions. You are trying to figure out how much money **really** is needed. You are not trying to get that number to zero with a fantasy set of assumptions.

I cannot stress enough the importance of making sure you don't change your assumptions simply to reduce the money needed by the business. It's easy to change the assumptions but

	Jan	Feb	March	April	May	June	July	Aug	Sept	Oct	Nov
Operating Cash Inflows											
Cash Sales	$10,000	$14,000	$16,000	$18,000	$21,000	$24,000	$27,000	$33,000	$39,000	$48,000	$57,000
Total Operating Cash Inflows	10,000	14,000	16,000	18,000	21,000	24,000	27,000	33,000	39,000	48,000	57,000
Operating Cash Outflows											
Purchases	5,000	7,000	8,000	9,000	10,500	12,000	13,500	16,500	19,500	24,000	28,500
Payroll	4,500	4,500	5,500	5,500	6,500	6,500	7,500	7,500	7,500	8,500	8,500
Other Operating Expenses	5,500	6,000	7,000	7,000	7,500	8,000	8,500	8,500	8,500	8,500	8,500
Total Operating Cash Outflows	15,000	17,500	20,500	21,500	24,500	26,500	29,500	32,500	35,500	41,000	45,500
Net Operating Cash Flow	(5,000)	(3,500)	(4,500)	(3,500)	(3,500)	(2,500)	(2,500)	500	3,500	7,000	11,500
Non Operating Inflows/Outflows											
Add:											
Beginning Cash Balance	0	20,000	16,500	12,000	8,500	5,000	2,500	0	500	4,000	11,000
Money Invested (Equity)	25,000										
Money Borrowed (Debt)											
Subtract:											
Debt Repayment											
Interest Payments											
Taxes											
Total Non Operating Inflows/Outflows	25,000	20,000	16,500	12,000	8,500	5,000	2,500	0	500	4,000	11,000
Ending Cash Balance	$20,000	$16,500	$12,000	$8,500	$5,000	$2,500	$0	$500	$4,000	$11,000	$22,500

( ) Means negative number

Revised Cash Flow Statement

Figure 7–5

you can't change the reality. So, **if the assumptions you make are not realistic, you will find yourself in the position many unfortunate entrepreneurs wind up in—running out of money and having their business fail.**

However, some assumptions can be changed realistically. The most obvious is to use another business concept. Remember, our cash flow statement is the way to compare the cost of alternative business concepts. If one concept clearly costs too much, then try another concept. Of course, as I mentioned, the lowest-cost concept is not always the best, but cost is an extremely important factor. However, once you've settled on a business concept, you can still lower costs. For example, you may be able to raise the price of your product or service or spend less on salaries and wages or lower production costs. A really skilled negotiator can usually negotiate lower rents, better deals from suppliers, and perhaps, prompter payment from customers.

When Ruth Owades started her first business, Gardener's Eden, she was very successful in a number of skillful negotiations:[1]

> She leased office space at a very low rate; she held out for a 3% charge for credit card processing; she arranged for no deposits for utilities or telephone; she obtained long term credit terms from suppliers of catalog items. She also introduced herself, her background, and her plans to Dun & Bradstreet and got a favorable report issued which greatly helped her obtain the other results.

In addition, one word of warning: When it comes to costs, it's very easy to spend, particularly on something you love; and because the business you're in or planning is something you love, it's easy to overspend. Every time it comes to laying out hard earned cash, examine the benefit to your customer. If it doesn't directly benefit your customer or if it's not **extremely** important to the business, don't spend the money. Don't think twice about spending money. Think three times.

[1]Richard O. von Wersowetz, Robert Kent, and Howard Stevenson, "Ruth M. Owades," Harvard Business School, 9-383-051 (Boston: Harvard College, 1982, rev. 2/85).

COMPUTERS AND CASH FLOWS

Now that you have a better understanding of the mechanics of cash flow preparation, I want to say a few words about using technology to assist in this process. When I started my first business in 1973, I was happy to have a calculator. At that time, there was no such thing as microcomputers. But there was a positive side of having to pick up a pencil and paper and work out the numbers. It helped me develop an understanding of how cash flow statements related to my decisions, and that information helped me develop a feel for my business. Obviously, the downside was that it took a lot of time, so I was reluctant to keep changing my assumptions and therefore did not consider as many alternative business concepts as I should have.

Today, thanks to the microcomputer and dozens of software programs designed specifically to generate cash flows, you can quickly prepare a cash flow statement and, with just a few keystrokes, run out as many alternative sets of assumptions as you desire.[2] Remember, even though the numbers now can be prepared using sophisticated software, they are just as dependent on the validity of your assumptions as hand-generated numbers. The problem is that laser-printed output looks so good you almost forget that, if your assumptions are wrong, your cash flow statements are wrong. So, use the technology to assist you, but make sure you fully understand what the cash flow statement tells you and make sure you are realistic about all of your assumptions.

COST VERSUS FLEXIBILITY

However, as I said, cost is not the only factor to consider. For instance, one of your main goals is to maintain as much flexibility as possible. Flexibility allows you to change quickly should the current cycle of customer interaction indicate the need. For exam-

---

[2] I know I'm biased, but Ronstadt's Financials is the best software program for quickly generating accurate cash flow statements. In fact, Ronstadt's Financials will allow you to gain control over all of your critical financial decisions. Enough said, let's get back to the task at hand.

ple, let's assume that, from your most recent customer interaction cycle, you realize you need a piece of equipment in your manufacturing process that allows for greater customization of your product. The piece of equipment costs $50,000. One option is to buy the equipment and finance its purchase through your bank. Another option is to rent the machine on a monthly basis. However, the monthly rental figure is very high as compared to buying the machine and financing its purchase through your bank. But the monthly cost is not the only factor. You also need to think about which option gives you the greatest flexibility. Think what would happen, if during your next customer interaction cycle, you determine that your customers really do not want the product as you are producing it and you must take a totally new approach, maybe even do away with the product completely. What are you going to do with your $50,000 piece of equipment, send it to the bank? Thus, paying more to rent may be much better than buying, because now you can simply stop renting. Sure, you could try to sell the machine. But, until you sell it, you don't have the cash to use for your next customer interaction cycle. So, although I am not advocating renting, you should be clear that every business decision has implications that must be explored.

Look at what Eyal Balle does to maintain flexibility as he's building his $7 million shoe business, Rebels:[3]

> He recalls, "I didn't want to commit to a warehouse. . . . Warehouse owners want five-year leases." He settled on Public Storage as his landlord. Balle never signed a long-term lease for the warehouse space, preferring to pay an extra $100 a month for the right to break his lease. It proved a wise move, since Rebels is about to move into its fifth warehouse in three years.

CLOSE TO THE BUSINESS OR
CLOSE TO THE CUSTOMER

In addition to flexibility, another compelling criterion to consider is whether an item is "close" to the customer or "close" to

[3]Edward O. Welles, "Basic Instincts," *Inc.* (September 1996), pp. 38–50.

the business. If you remember, when Tim DeMello was deciding whether to rent or buy a delivery van, he chose to buy because he could paint it with his logo and it was the one part of his business that his customers saw. In other words, it was "close" to his customers. But he rented or leased his own offices and much of the equipment in them because it was "close" to his business. It made absolutely no difference to his customer. He and his employees were the only ones who saw them.

It is much more effective to invest limited money resources in the areas that make the most difference to the customer. Whenever you look at costs in each of your alternative business concepts, you'll see that some costs are "close" to the customer, like advertising and product packaging, whereas other costs are "close" to the business, like manufacturing equipment and the rent paid for your offices. More weight always must be given to items that are "close" to the customer. I've lost count of the number of times I've met with an executive at his or her lavish office when I knew the executive was desperately looking for money. It's one thing if customers come to your office, but if it's just your office, it's a mistake. Those investments in fancy offices might turn out to mean the difference between a business's survival and bankruptcy.

Once you've completed your cash flow statements for a variety of alternative business concepts and have included those results along with such factors as the degree of flexibility and the closeness of the investments to your customers, you now need to decide which business concept to use. If you think the decision still is difficult, you're right. But, regardless, you must make the choice. In Chapters 8 and 9, we discuss a few more criteria for making your decision. However, for the moment, let me emphasize that, even after considering all the "facts," the ultimate determining factor always is your "intuitive feeling," which again is why loving your business is so important: **Loving your business increases your intuitive ability to feel your business and make the right choices.** But, even if your intuition is off, if you follow the rhythm of business, understand that every customer interaction cycle is a learning process, and are prepared to change, in your next customer interaction cycle, you can make the necessary adjustments and transform the wrong choice into the right choice.

GETTING THE MONEY YOU NEED—BANKS

Since this is a chapter on money, let's now turn to where and how you get the money to fill the gaps between your cash inflow from sales and your cash outflow from expenses. Whether your business is large or small, money can be loaned to or invested in the business. Most likely, you have heard or read about how difficult it is for existing businesses, let alone new businesses, to get a bank loan. Unfortunately, what you've heard or read is true. Despite what bank advertisements claim, banks don't like loaning money to what they perceive as risky investments; and to a bank, a new business always is a risky investment. When Jim Koch, brewer of Samuel Adams and Boston Lager, was starting his company, he raised $400,000 ($100,000 from his savings and $300,000 from friends and relatives) because "no banks would lend him money to build a small brewery."[4] Tim Jemison had the same experience with his company, Online Scouting Network LLC, formed to allow colleges to recruit high school athletes over the Internet. "We sat down with four or five banks, and they all said they didn't want anything to do with a start-up. . . . They said they lend on results, not projections."[5]

Inc. magazine agrees. Here's its description of what it's like trying to get a loan from a bank for a new business.[6]

> In a discussion of the galaxy of financial resources available to young companies, one myth dies especially hard: that commercial bankers have a fundamental interest in making loans to start-

[4]Michael Saunders, "Brewing *up a* Storm," *The Boston Globe Magazine* (November 10, 1996), p. 57.
[5]Gianna Jacobson, "Money Hunter Mindset," *Success* (November 1996), p. 35.
[6]Bruce G. Posner, "How to Finance Anything," *Inc.* (February 1993), p. 54. Excerpted with permission, *Inc.* magazine (February 1993). Copyright by Goldhirsh Group, Inc., 38 Commercial Wharf, Boston, MA 02110.

up businesses. True, a lot of bankers refrain from closing the door on owners of early-stage companies too abruptly. Many, in fact, will dutifully flip through your business plan and talk with you about what you need. But when the chips are down, you won't find many of them prepared to make *business* loans to companies younger than three or four years old. That's especially true today, with industry regulators monitoring banks so tightly. The loans banks do make (ostensibly to companies) are almost always collateralized by homes and other personal assets.

Contrary to what many start-ups wish were true, that practice isn't about to change even if banks begin to loosen up and increase their lending over the months and years ahead. Bankers can't afford to act like venture capitalists, because of the way they're capitalized and regulated. While both bankers and venture capitalists deal in money, Alex Sheshunoff, president of Alex Sheshunoff Management Services, a consultant to banks in Austin, Texas, notes, "When a bank wins, it makes 4% over its costs of money. And when it loses, it can lose everything, plus attorney's fees." So a banker is judged, first and foremost, on his or her ability to get the money back. Recession or no recession, credit crunch or not, the key questions for a banker are 1) what's the borrower's track record, and 2) if we lend the money, how will we be repaid? The typical young company owner's answers go a long way toward explaining why bankers are seldom keen about lending to early-stage businesses.

As you can see, even if you coax a bank into making a loan to your business, the bank usually will ask you to guarantee the loan with hard assets, which means, if your business is unable to repay the loan, the bank will take over the assets. If your business is new and has no hard assets, the bank will want you to personally guarantee the loan with whatever hard assets you have, which usually means your home. And, I can tell you, banks play hardball. They really do want their money back and will exercise all legal recourse to make sure they get it, even if they have to sell **your** house. Just ask Bill Rodgers, the noted marathoner and one-time owner of Bill Rodgers & Co. (a producer of BR running gear). When his business ran into problems Rodgers couldn't believe that the bank wanted his home but it did and the bank got it:[7]

---

[7]Joseph P. Kahn, "Heartbreak Hill," *Inc.* (April 1988), pp. 68–78.

> After weeks of negotiations, Rodgers concluded a settlement with the Bank of Boston. Under the terms of the agreement, the bank purchased his house in Dover [Massachusetts] in exchange for the extinguishing of his remaining indebtedness.

I'm not saying all this to discourage potential entrepreneurs. However, in most instances, a business has to obtain the money it needs by having people make equity investments. And, if it's your business, as you'd expect, the very first person to invest has to be you. After all, it's your business, and if you're not willing to make an investment, no one else will. This may sound obvious. But when you sit down and write out a check payable to your new business, you will get a much better understanding of the commitment required and the commitment required of investors who do not love your business as deeply as you do. (A real advantage of starting small with a low-cost concept is that it reduces the amount of cash needed and increases the likelihood that you can finance your first customer interaction cycle yourself. And as stressed in Chapter 2, your objective is to get to the profitable level of operation as quickly as possible, thereby reducing the need for outside financing.)

EQUITY INVESTORS

However, even in the case of small businesses, after you've written your own check, you most likely still will need to raise more cash. In that case, you need to sell equity investments. At the time a business is started, the founders own 100 percent of the company. But when someone makes an equity investment, he or she does so for a percentage of the business. In essence, the owner sells a piece of the business in return for cash. But how much of the business for how much cash? Although there are some general rules, the process inevitably boils down to negotiation. It therefore is very important to be a good negotiator and understand how an outside investor thinks.

Investors rightly believe that, the greater is the perceived risk, the greater the percentage of the business that must be sold.

For example, if you are starting a business and need to raise $100,000 and the investor feels there is a lot of risk, the investor will want a large percentage of your business for each dollar invested. However, if the investor feels the risk is less (or viewed more positively, if the investor feels that the chances of success are greater), the investor will expect to receive less of your company for each dollar invested. So what, you might say, as long as I get the money. Well, that can be a very expensive "so what." Down the road, the 5 percent of your company you don't have to sell could turn out to represent a sizable amount of cash. Plus, each time you sell a piece of your business, you are selling a piece of the control. So, how much equity you have to sell is important for your own future financial reward as well as for control of your business. But, because in most businesses, whether old or new, you do have to sell some equity, it's important to make your business look as risk free as possible, which is another reason why I have spent so much time explaining how to create a cash flow statement. Generating a cash flow forecast for each customer interaction cycle helps lower the perception and the reality of risk. Structuring your cycles so that each one ends with the accomplishment of clearly identifiable goals shows increased understanding of your customer and points a clear path toward a profitable business. As the level of risk comes down, the overall value of your business increases and the percentage of your company an investor requires is reduced. Thus, by following the rhythm of business, not only do you stand a better chance of success, but you wind up owning more of your business. **The rhythm of business is based on knowledge of your customers, and knowledge of your customers reduces risk**. It is a clear, practical point, and if you can see it, investors can, too.

SHUMAN'S BONANZA

To help better understand how these equity issues play out, let's put together some figures for a possible business. Let's call the business Shuman's Bonanza and track it through three customer interaction cycles. When I first start the business, I personally invest $50,000 in the company by purchasing 5 million shares of common stock at $.01 per share. This stock, often referred to as *founder's stock*, generally is purchased by the founder(s) at a low per share price. Actually, stock bought at a penny a share has value only if later you are able to get people to buy stock in the company at a higher price per share. Because I own all of the stock of the company, the overall valuation of Shuman's Bonanza is $50,000 ($0.01/share x 5 million shares).

At the time I prepare a cash flow statement and business plan for my first customer interaction cycle, I determine I need approximately $250,000, which I raise by selling approximately 384,615 shares of the company at $0.65 per share. Notice what happens now to the overall valuation of my company. After the cycle 1 funding is raised, 5,384,615 shares of Shuman's Bonanza are outstanding with a value of $0.65/share, because all outstanding shares are valued at the most recent per-share price. Therefore, the valuation for Shuman's Bonanza has increased from the $50,000 level to approximately $3.5 million.

For each of the next two customer interaction cycles, let's say I follow the same process as reflected in Table 7–1.

TABLE 7–1

Cycle Number	New Shares Sold	Per-Share Price	Money Raised	Approximate Valuation
Founder's	5,000,000	$0.01	$50,000	$50,000
1	384,615	$0.65	$250,000	$3,500,000
2	500,000	$0.80	$400,000	$4,707,692
3	361,111	$0.90	$325,000	$5,621,153
Totals	6,245,726		$1,025,000	

As can be seen in Table 7–1, after the fourth round (including the founder's stock round) of cycle-based funding, $1,025,000 has been raised by selling 6,245,726 shares in three private placement rounds at an average price per share of $0.16. Due to the last sale price per share of $0.90, Shuman's Bonanza valuation has increased to approximately $5.6 million dollars (6,245,726 shares x $0.90/share). And, of this, my 5 million shares now have a value of approximately $4.5 million. Obviously, this is a "paper value" because there is no public market for Shuman's Bonanza stock. The $4.5 million is not in my personal bank account that I can spend. That $4.5 million dollars is only a theoretical paper value, based on the number of shares I own at the most recent price per share that I have found an investor willing to pay. Until I either sell Shuman's Bonanza to another business or sell part of the company to the public through an initial public offering, all I have is a valuation on paper.

But, the cash from the $1.025 million worth of stock that I've sold is real, and I now can invest it in my business. At the end of the third round of financing, assuming approximately 50 individuals have made investments in me and Shuman's Bonanza, that means on average each investor has invested approximately $20,000 in my business.

One of the interesting aspects of raising money from investors is that they inevitably are friendly with other investors. So, if you can get one to invest, they usually introduce you to their circle of investor friends, who also make investments. And, not surprisingly, many of those investors also have their own circle of friends who in turn may invest more money. So, knowing one investor may ultimately lead to dozens of potential investors and hundreds of thousands of dollars.

THE ONE WHO HAS THE GOLD RULES

You might wonder how I determined that the price per share for the first cycle should be $0.65 and that it could be increased to $0.80 for cycle 2 and $0.90 for cycle 3. As mentioned previously, there are no set rules for determining the asking price per share for a privately held company. In fact, you essentially can set whatever price you want. The key, however, is to get people to invest at the price set, so realism is important and this is one instance in which the "golden rule" clearly applies. Only in this case the golden rule is "the one who has the gold rules," which means that, because the investors have the money (the gold), they have significant leverage when negotiating the exchange rate.

Although in this example the money is successfully raised, the business of raising money is far from done. In fact, now that I've finished three cycles of customer interaction and have my business on steady footing, I'm ready to expand and need to raise, let's say, another $2 million dollars, which is more money than I've raised in all three initial startup cycles. And after this first business expansion, I'll need to raise several millions of dollars more as I open more offices throughout the state. When Shuman's Bonanza goes national, I'll again need millions of dollars. At each level of expansion I have to do exactly the same things as I did when I was trying to raise the money needed for the first cycle of customer interaction. I have to gather all the relevant information, make the necessary assumptions, prepare a cash flow, and then find investors willing to invest their money in my business. So, as you can see, raising money can be an ongoing process throughout the life of your business.

Let me go back to the quote at the beginning of the chapter: "Happiness is a positive cash flow." Fred Adler's right. Until the operating cash flow of a business is positive, that is, until a business generates more cash than it spends, you continually have to focus on raising money to sustain and grow the company. As raising money is a difficult, time-consuming, and often humbling process, you want to achieve a positive operating cash flow as quickly as possible.

YOUR BUSINESS PLAN

Accompanying your cash flow statement, investors or senior management also will want to see a business plan. In fact, it is unlikely today that you can find any investor or bank to invest or loan a business money without first seeing a business plan.

Although business plans come in all sizes and shapes, a typical business plan is a document of approximately 25 to 30 pages and covers the following topics:

- **Summary Information.** Usually a one-page summary of the marketplace opportunity, the customers' wants and needs, the business concept, management, and the money (capital) needed. This is the most important page in the plan, because its objective is to get the investor or senior management to read the rest of your plan.
- **Risk Factors.** This one- to two-page section highlights the key risks inherent in the business. The purpose of this section is not to scare away investors but to show that you have evaluated the business realistically and identified critical factors that both you and outside investors should take into consideration.
- **The Company.** You next present a one- to two-page overview of the company's business concept and strategy, detailing what the company is trying to accomplish and how it intends to accomplish it.
- **The Industry.** This two- to four-page section describes the overall industry structure, identifies the key trends having an impact on the industry, and profiles key competitors.
- **The Business.** This four- to six-page section describes in some detail the company's mission, its business concept and strategy, product or service offerings, significant milestones, and opportunities for future growth. Remember, the attainment of these milestones should reduce an investor's perception of the risk involved, thereby increasing the value of the business.
- **Marketing.** This three- to five-page section describes the company's anticipated marketing program: pricing strategy, promotional activities, distribution channels, and most important, its overall marketplace positioning. The positioning statement is key because, in essence, it provides your customers' reason for buying your product or service.

- **Operations.** This three- to five-page section provides an overview of the company's planned operations strategy and information systems.
- **Management.** This section of three to five pages describes the company's management team, board of directors, employees, and organizational structure. You want to show clearly that you and your team can do what needs to be done for the business to be successful. For many investors, this is the key section of the plan, because such investors feel they are not really betting on the business per se but on the "jockey"—you and the management team.
- **Description of Capital Stock.** This one-page section provides an overview of the company's stock, its stock dividend policy, and stock option plans (if any).
- **Capital Needs.** This one- to two-page section identifies the amount of funding sought and how those dollars are to be used.
- **Financial Information.** This two- to three-page section highlights the company's financial history (if any) and summarizes its cash flow projections.[8]
- **Appendices.** This section includes whatever other information you feel may be of value to the potential investor.

Business plans are good because, as with a cash flow statement, they share with investors the information you have about your customers as well as how your business is going to satisfy those customers and thus reduces the perceived riskiness of the business. They also give a convenient written description of your business that can precede you when you meet senior management or any potential investor or lender. Thereby, they serve as a marketing vehicle for your ideas and for your "investor shopping."

Actually, even if you are starting a business that requires no outside money (beyond your own investment), you should still

---

[8]Although I have focused on the preparation of the cash flow statement, because it allows you to determine how much money is needed and when it will be needed, you should also prepare a proforma (projected) balance sheet and profit and loss statement for every customer interaction cycle.

prepare a business plan. A business plan forces you to gather, process, and connect as much information as you can about your customers and your business. It is one of the first steps in making your vision of your company more concrete. As a result, it is a very important document, even if you are the only one going to read it.

Since I recommend that you prepare your cash flow projections on a cycle by cycle basis, you should prepare a revised business plan for each cycle. As your understanding of your customers and the business concept best able to satisfy those customers increases after each cycle, you need to reflect your new understanding in your business plan. Although this may seem like a lot of extra work, it really isn't. In many instances, it involves just updating what already is in the plan. What, at first, you may regard as extra work will prove its worth many times over and become standard operating procedure. Why? Because having to rewrite your business plan focuses your thinking on step 4, analysis and refinement, which is a very important step in the rhythm of business. Here, you see what you are doing right, what you are doing wrong, and figure out how to correct what's wrong.

All too often businesspeople prepare only one business plan. Then they put on their "blinders" and concentrate solely on bringing that business to life. As mentioned in Chapter 6, they seek no additional information, are uninterested in changes, and therefore do not modify their thinking based on an increased understanding of their customers; and more often than not, their businesses fail. Having to rewrite your business plan with each customer interaction cycle ensures that you will do the analyzing and refining your business requires. Psychologically, it also ensures that flexibility and change are part of your thinking right from the start. If you know you'll be writing a new business plan for each cycle, you will not put on blinders.

SOURCES OF FUNDING

After preparing your cash flow statement and your business plan, if you own your own business, where do you find the investors to show these documents? That's a really important question and has been the subject of dozens of books on how to finance a new business. For our purposes, I identified and briefly described the usual sources of financing, listed in the sequence they are best approached:

- **Your Own Money.** As discussed, your own money is the first cash invested. The money usually comes from personal savings and, increasingly, from cash advances from credit cards. When outside investors look at your business, they usually are not concerned with the amount of your investment in an absolute sense. Rather, they consider your investment in relation to their estimate of your net worth. They want to make sure you have enough money invested that, if things get tough, as they inevitably do, you will not "walk" away from the business. I know the thought of walking away from your business may seem unimaginable now, but believe me, when that roller coaster is heading toward the bottom, there are going to be times you wish you could walk away, and outside investors want to make sure you have every incentive to stay.
- **Family and Friends.** It is comparatively easy to get money from family and friends, because they usually make the investment because of their relationship rather than as a result of having carefully evaluated your business. However, although that approach is helpful when it comes to getting the money, you must realize that taking money from family and friends oftentimes puts your relationship at risk. Listen to how Ruth Owades feels about having friends invest in her businesses:[9] "I never asked friends to invest, although a number did come to me with, 'I have $30,000 to invest' or 'I have $50,000.' I thought about it and was very touched, but decided no. The possibility was that I would lose the money for them—and the friendship was

[9]von Wersowetz et al., 1982, p. 5.

too important." From experience, I can tell you it doesn't matter that you, too, lost money or that you worked hard to make a go of the business. In the end, all that matters is that **you lost their money**. So remember "friendly" money might be easy to get, but your family and friends expect to get their money back.

- **Wealthy Individuals.** This category of investors, often called *informal investors* or *angels*, is made up of wealthy individuals who enjoy investing in startup companies. As such, you often find the list of investors includes doctors, lawyers, entrepreneurs, and other individuals who have accumulated a sizable net worth. The reason these investors are considered "informal" is because they do not make investments as their primary business activity. Consequently, it often is difficult to locate these people. Fortunately, over the past several years, more and more programs and organizations composed of these investors have come into existence. Magazines like *Success* and *Inc.* and Web sites on the Internet publish listings of informal investor organizations. Although it is very difficult to get an accurate figure on the amount of money this group invests on an annual basis, it has been estimated that, in the United States alone, the amount is over $20 billion, which means that, in aggregate, this group invests more in new businesses than any other group.

- **Strategic Alliance Partners.** As discussed in the last chapter, strategic alliances increasingly are utilized by those building and running businesses. And, in many instances, businesses are turning to their alliance "partners" as sources of venture funding. Even though there are almost as many different types of funding arrangements (such as exchanges of goods for services or long-term payback plans) as there are alliances, it is not surprising to find that many new businesses have received funding from suppliers or customers with whom they have structured alliances.

- **Venture Capital Firms.** These are professionally managed venture funds that make investments in startups and latter-stage businesses. Unfortunately, unless your business has the potential of growing to at least $50 million in annual revenue in five years, it is highly unlikely a venture capital firm will find your business of interest. Because these firms are in the investment business, it is easy to obtain a listing of who they are from your local library. Despite their name, these firms tend to prefer later-round financing in which the risks of venture failure have (ideally) been reduced. In the United States, venture capital firms annually invest approximately $10 billion. I should point out that, if you are inside a large existing business, you usually wind up going to your company's CFO for the money needed. Every company will have its own unique capital budgeting process, but getting money from the CFO, in most respects, is very similar to getting money from venture capitalists. Although your CFO most likely expects a lower implicit rate of return on invested capital than a venture capitalist, CFOs allocate money to a number of "competing" projects, and you have to demonstrate the worth of your project to a CFO, using the same criteria as you would to any outside investor.

- **Initial Public Offering.** Going public is the process by which a business owned by one or several individuals is converted into a business owned by many. It involves offering part ownership of the company to the public through the sale of equity or debt securities and is closely regulated by the Securities and Exchange Commission (SEC). Although it is possible to take a new business public when you are first starting out, usually taking a company "public" is the pot of gold at the end of, at least, a few years of successful operation. The other pot of gold is to "cash out" by selling the company to another business or group of investors.

Although the preceding list does not enumerate every funding source, it identifies the key sources. When it comes to funding a business, more than any other quality, you need to be resource-ful. To start and run a business requires imaginative thinking and hard and seemingly constant work. But it can be done.

Here's another word of caution. If you are selling part of your business, even to a friend or relative, think about what it will be like to have that person as an investor. It's almost like asking yourself whether you would want to be "married" to that person, because once you've sold someone an interest in your business, it is no longer just **your** business. Investors don't go away. They want to be involved, some more than others; but they all like to keep a watchful eye on what you do with **their money**. Of course, this has a good side as well as a bad. Knowl-edgeable investors can provide a great benefit to a business beyond their money. Perhaps they have key customer or sup-plier contacts, or maybe they possess special skills or expertise you could utilize. And, having invested money in your com-pany, these investors now have a major incentive to help in as many ways as possible.

THE DANCERS

At this point, since this chapter is entitled "Raising Money *and* Motivating People," let's focus on the other critical resource needed to build a successful business—people. Depending on the size of a business, one or more people may be involved. Of course, how many and what type of people depends on the par-ticular business. Nonetheless, several people questions are com-mon to all businesses.

If you are hiring for your own business or your company, one of the first issues is to identify the type of people needed and how to find them. As with money needs, particularly with a new business, you should look at your people requirements on a cycle-by-cycle basis, because your needs may change as you refine your business concept after each customer interaction cycle.

For example, when looking toward cycle 1 of a new busi-ness, identify the skills and expertise needed to carry out that cycle. You are just starting, so try to do as much yourself as you can. Determine whether you have the capability for each task required. If you do and you believe you will have the time, then don't bring someone else into the business. However, if you lack the ability or the time, then you must get someone. Depending on your financial resources, you basically have the option of bringing someone in as a working partner or an employee on either a full or part-time basis, or you may be able to outsource the activity to some other company, perhaps through a strategic alliance as Paul Farrow did when he started Walden Paddlers.

DANCE PARTNERS

Let's first look at the option of bringing in a working partner. Partners are individuals that, like you, have made an equity investment and work in the business. In some instances, you may decide that you need to put together an "entrepreneurial team" of people. Very often informal investors and venture capital firms require that you have partners as a condition for their investment. It's felt that a business with partners is less risky than a business founded by a lone individual. Investors are rightly concerned about what might happen to your business and their money if something happens to you. However, more than any other people issue, taking on a partner or a team of partners fundamentally changes your business. It is no longer your business, rather it has become **our business**. As a result, your ability to do what you want is severely limited.

However, if you decide to bring in a partner or partners (and it is a big decision), be sure that you discuss your business and your business goals with them thoroughly. It's more important to share business philosophies than to be friends with your partner. Friendships change but philosophies of life, ideas of how you conduct yourself, and how you want your business to be conducted are much more fixed and much more important in a business relationship. Certainly, you want your partner to understand and believe in the rhythm of business. It will be of no use trying to conduct your business by the principles of the rhythm of business if your partner or partners do not share them. Your next customer interaction cycle may lead to a fundamental change in your business, and your partner needs to see that as well as you. Your partner needs to share your passion for your business and your dedication to information, flexibility, hard work, and your customer. Unfortunately, these are rarer qualities than you think. But your partner or partners must have them.

ASSEMBLING THE TROUPE

After deciding whether to bring in a partner, you still may need additional people. But, before hiring any full-time employees, whether it's your own company or you are a manager of a large corporation, consider again whether the potential employees share your own and your company's business philosophy. After all, employees are a vital part of a business and to large extent make it go; therefore, as with potential partners, select employees who understand the need for dedication to the customer, information, flexibility, and hard work and who also love the business you're in with a passion. They will need all these qualities to make the business successful, particularly if the business is a startup. With startups, employees often have to work long hours, wear two or more hats, and go the extra mile for customers. Yet the compensation usually is less and not as guaranteed as in an established company. So, before you make any compromises, consider using part-time help. Part-time employees may lack the needed personal qualities, but at the very least, they are inherently flexible, just by the nature of their employment, and can fill in until you find the right person. If a part-timer doesn't work out or you need someone else with different skills, a part-timer is much easier to replace than a full-time employee. As a result of an alliance, it also may be possible to get one of your alliance companies to provide the needed people for a specific project. So, be in no rush to hire people. But, if you do hire someone who turns out to be wrong, do not hesitate to let that person go. Keeping around an employee who doesn't fit in is bad for your business and bad for the employee.

THE PRINCIPAL DANCERS

In addition to the right personal qualities, in general, you want individuals who, in prior work situations, have demonstrated that they possess the capabilities needed. Bringing in people who have to learn on the job is a luxury most business can't afford. However, people who have a proven track record generally are more costly than those without prior experience. But, if they also have the right personal qualities, experienced employees are worth the expense, even if it causes some financial strain. However, if you have to choose between people with the right skills and people with the right personal qualities, choose the people with the right personal qualities. They can learn the necessary skills more quickly than those with the skills can gain the right personal qualities, which, in reality, may never happen.

One of the biggest mistakes a businessperson can make is to hire a particular employee because he or she is less costly. Although we have emphasized the importance of keeping costs low, saving a few dollars by bringing in a questionable person is the wrong way to save. If the person does not have the right personal qualities or the ability to do what needs to be done, your entire business may be at risk. In many situations you simply don't get a second chance. Consequently, you need to make sure you bring in the best person for the job.

If you have limited financial resources, once you find the right person, how do you persuade that person to join your company? This is a complex question for which there is no one answer, each individual is to some extent unique and has to be dealt with on a case-by-case basis, but one thing we can say is that the ability to negotiate plays a key role in hiring. Some of the items to be negotiated are job responsibilities, evaluation criteria, and the compensation package.

In particular, new businesses often are looked at by skilled people as opportunities to widen their job experiences or to work for stock options. Basically, stock options give the recipient the opportunity to purchase stock (an ownership interest) in the company at a preset option price. For example, they may have the option to buy 10,000 shares of the company's common stock at $2 per share. If, in the future, the company goes public and if the stock price increases to say $35 per share, the holder of the option could exercise the option, buy the stock from the company for $2 per share, and then sell it on the open market at $35 per share, which is not such a bad deal. Consider the situation at Microsoft, where more than 2,000 of its employees have become millionaires:[10]

> Leaving officers and directors aside (and that includes Mr. Gates and co-founder Paul Allen), 10,000 rank-and-file employees have almost 50 million vested options for stock worth over $3 billion.

In addition to partners and employees, other key people resources are a Board of Directors (if the business is organized as a corporation), an accountant, and a lawyer. Without question, here your overall objective is to surround yourself with the most experienced people, people whose opinions you value. As with so much else that comes into play in business, you have to make every possible effort to get good information the first time you ask for it. Consequently, you don't want someone to serve in these critical advisory capacities based on any criteria other than competence.

THE STREAMLINE ORGANIZATION

Now, let's look briefly at a few practical examples of how Tim DeMello handled his people needs. After incorporating in 1993, Tim put together a Board of Directors to assist him in developing Streamline. In addition to Tim, the board consists of four outside company directors. Tim also sketched out an organization chart for Streamline identifying the key positions that had to be filled

---

[10]Dan Lavin, "Millionaires @ Work," *Fortune* (April 3, 1995).

as the company worked its way through its first four customer interaction cycles. As can be seen in Figure 7–6, Tim envisioned a structure that had four managerial positions that oversaw the three key processes that were focused on the customer.

Shortly after starting the company, Tim hired an assistant responsible for helping him run the office. In preparation for cycle 1 testing, Tim brought in two additional employees, one to work in the office and one to drive the dry cleaning pickup/delivery van. Tim and these three employees were able to handle cycles 1 and 2. However, as Streamline made the transition into cycle 3, Tim had to increase his personnel to assist with the growing number of operational activities and to meet with the growing number of outside (informal) investors. So, Tim added five people to the Streamline family. By the start of cycle 4, the company had 12 employees, 9 working full-time (including the four in managerial positions) and 3 part-time. In connection with the opening of his prototype Customer Resource Center in cycle 5, Tim had to hire additional marketing, sales, systems, and operations employees.

Tim also put together an outside Advisory Board to aid him in planning the company's growth. Given his plans to take Streamline public sometime in the future, Tim always has sought the best legal and accounting assistance. He appreciates that he is paying more than he has to for his legal and accounting work, since Streamline is still a small company, but Tim nevertheless believes that the extra outlay is money well spent. Given his early background as a stockbroker, Tim knows all too well the problems a company can face going public if it has not received the best advice early on.

In view of the company's continuing financing needs, Tim has been particularly careful in putting together the compensation packages that are required to get the right people. Because of his uncompromising vision for Streamline, Tim has focused on bringing in the best people possible. However, to get these people, Tim has used compensation packages with current and deferred elements, including generous stock option plans for key employees and directors.

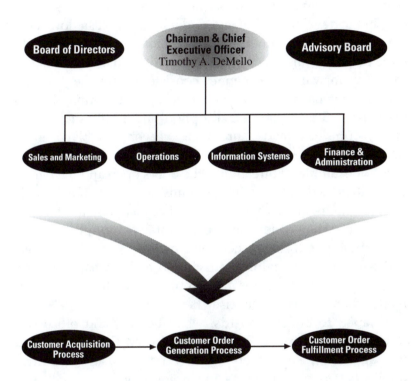

Organizational Structure
(Streamline, Inc.)
Figure 7–6

Knowing the critical role the "right" culture plays in the survival and growth of a new business, Tim also makes sure that he does whatever is necessary to foster the kind of work environment he wants. For instance, all of Tim's employees participate in the development of and understand the cash flow model the company uses with each of its customer interaction cycles. Each employee also appreciates his or her role in moving the company forward in a manner consistent with the cash flow assumptions used in the model. And, most important, by carefully using Streamline's stock option and profit sharing programs, Tim has made sure that everyone involved in the company has a vested interest in Streamline's success.

For example, at Streamline, the doors open and the parking lot is full at 6:30 A.M., and it is not unusual that people are still at work 12 hours later. They do it, not because they are forced to but because they believe in and are totally committed to what the company is trying to accomplish. They share Tim's dream and want to do everything possible to make it happen. That's why they work 60 to 70 or more hours a week for probably less money than they could get elsewhere.

Taped to bulletin boards, white boards, and office walls throughout Streamline is the motto Every Day Counts. This message helps keep everyone focused on using time (and, implicitly, money) wisely. As an employee of Streamline, everyone is encouraged to get the most out of every single day.

Now that we've taken a general look at the key issues of money and people, it's time to shift our focus and take a look at what is one of the most important factors in building and running a company—keeping your eye on the details.

KEY POINTS IN CHAPTER 7

• As you work your way toward the ideal business, customer interaction cycle after customer interaction cycle, you need to assemble and reassemble your resources to accommodate any changes.

• If you are going to build and run a successful business, you must be able to motivate the money and people resources around your vision.

• Unless **you** understand the financial impact of your business decisions, you will not feel the rhythm of business and you will not be successful in business.

• To prepare an accurate cash flow statement you must become comfortable making critical assumptions about your business, and to do that you need to gather accurate information.

• I suggest that you tie your cash flow statement to the length of time you plan for each customer interaction cycle.

• Conventional wisdom allows for the possibility of unseen circumstances such as a recession or competing technological breakthroughs but it still insists that a linear process leads to success.

• As Peter Drucker and Leo Kahn point out, the business described in your carefully written business plan is rarely the successful business that develops. Natural-born businesspeople instinctively recognize this, and although they may go through the conventional strategies of writing a business plan, intuitively they are more focused on the rhythm than the plan and always are ready to move with the beat, always ready to change.

• The old and often recommended cash flow methods tend to prevent flexibility and keep you wedded to your initial three- to five-year plan. This happens because, once those written estimates are in the hands of your backers (investors and bankers), any deviation from those plans becomes a danger sign that your business is failing rather than a vital sign that your business needs to change.

- I feel you are much better off to link your cash flow statements to your customer interaction cycles. However, as discussed in Chapter 2, because it is difficult to tell exactly how long a customer interaction cycle will last and you never want to run out of money, you should allow yourself a couple of months' leeway. For example, if you believe that the next interaction cycle will last 9 months, you should run out the cash flow for 11 months, just in case.

- Forecasting sales is the most important assumption you make in a cash flow, because it directly influences most of your other assumptions.

- It is much more effective to invest limited money resources in areas that make the most difference to the customer. Whenever you look at costs, you'll see that some are "close" to the customer, like advertising and product packaging, whereas others are "close" to the business, like manufacturing equipment and the rent paid for your offices. More weight always must be given to items that are "close" to the customer.

- Once you've completed your cash flow statements for a variety of alternative business concepts and have included those results along with such factors as the degree of flexibility and the closeness of the investments to your customers, you need to decide which business concept to use. However, even after considering all the "facts," the ultimate determining factor always is your "intuitive feeling," which is why loving your business is so important: **Loving your business increases your intuitive ability to feel your business and make the right choices**.

- Structuring your cycles so that each one ends with the accomplishment of clearly identifiable goals and shows increasing understanding of your customer points a clear path toward a profitable business.

• Until the operating cash flow of a business is positive, that is, until a business generates more cash than it spends, you continually have to focus on raising money to sustain and grow the company.

• A business plan forces you to gather, process, and connect as much information as you can about your customers and your business; and it is one of the first steps in making your vision of your company more concrete.

• I recommend that you prepare your cash flow projections on a cycle-by-cycle basis and prepare a revised business plan for each cycle. As your understanding of your customers and the business concept best able to satisfy those customers increases after each cycle, you need to reflect your new understanding in your business plan.

• Having to rewrite your business plan focuses your thinking on step 4, analysis and refinement, which is a very important step in the rhythm of business. Here, you see what you are doing right, what you are doing wrong, and figure out how to correct what's wrong.

• If you are selling part of your business, even to a friend or relative, think about what it will be like to have that person as an investor.

• If you are hiring for your own business or company, one of the first issues is to identify the type of people needed and how to find them. As with money needs, you should look at your people requirements on a cycle-by-cycle basis, because your needs may change as you refine your business concept after each customer interaction cycle.

• As you are starting, try to do as much yourself as you can. Determine whether you have the capability for each task required. If you do and believe you will have the time, then don't bring someone else into the business.

• If you lack the ability or the time, then you must get someone. Depending on your financial resources, you basically have the option of bringing in someone as a working partner or an employee on either a full- or part-time basis, or you may be able to outsource the activity to some other company, perhaps though a strategic alliance.

• It's more important to share business philosophies than to be friends with your partner. Friendships change but philosophies of life, ideas of how you conduct yourself, and how you want your business to be conducted are much more fixed and much more important in a business relationship.

• Certainly, you want your partner to understand and believe in the rhythm of business. It will be of no use trying to conduct your business by the principles of the rhythm of business if your partner or partners do not share them.

• If you have to choose between people with the right skills and people with the right personal qualities, choose the people with the right personal qualities. They can learn the necessary skills more quickly than those with the skills can gain the right personal qualities, which, in reality, may never happen.

• Other key people resources are a Board of Directors (if the business is organized as a corporation), an accountant, and a lawyer. Without question, here your overall objective is to surround yourself with the most experienced people. You don't want someone in these critical advisory capacities based on any criteria other than competence.

The mechanics of running a business are not very complicated when you get down to essentials. You have to make some stuff and sell it. That's about all there is, except for a few million details.

…JOHN L. MCCAFFERY

8

Choreographing the Dance: Vision and Details

In the rhythm of business, step 2 is preparation, and preparation is concerned with details. Of course, getting the details right is part of every step of doing business, but if you're starting a business, step 2 is where you concentrate on creating your product or service and your business concept. Or, if your business is already begun, step 2 is where you implement any refinements that you learned were necessary from your previous customer interaction cycle. But, although it's important to get every detail done, it's also important not to become so overwhelmed by the details that you lose sight of your vision. You need to strike a balance between the two because, as was said in Chapter 6, your vision creates reality and reality shapes your vision. The simple fact is reality is in the details.

What do I mean? Remember the last time you threw a party? Most likely, when you first got the idea for the party, you "pictured" yourself having a good time with people you care about. That was your vision. But, think for a moment about all the details that had to be done for the party to be a success. You had to decide when and where to have the party, who would be invited, what kind and how much food you would serve, what type of music you would play, and so on. I'm sure, if you wrote down all of the details, you'd have a pretty long list. And, in the back of your mind, you knew that forgetting even one seemingly minor item, like getting enough ice cubes, could influence whether the party was a success or failure. But, no matter how important it is to keep track of all the details, it is equally important to keep track of your vision. If your vision is of a costume party, all the details must support that vision. If your vision is of a casual affair, then all the details must support that vision. Let's say, to fulfill your vision, you budget $150. What happens if, when you start putting together all the details, you suddenly discover that certain items require a larger expenditure and your party budget mushrooms to $250. If you don't want to spend the $250, you will have to change the style of the party and the details then will change. Thus, we can see your vision creates the details (reality) and the details (reality) shape your vision. Further, you and your spouse have to share the same vision. If one of you buys items for a costume party and the other buys items for a casual affair, the evening could turn into a mess. Maybe, in the end, you, your spouse, and your guests have a good laugh over it, but in business, a mess like that is no laughing matter.

So, you need to strike a balance between the details and your vision, and if partners and employees are involved, you need to make sure it's a shared vision. With a shared vision, your company heads in one direction rather than in as many directions as you have partners and employees.

You've probably heard the expression, "Things always cost twice as much and take twice as long as you thought." Well, if you think about it, "things" really don't cost twice as much or take twice as long. What happens is that, because you focused on your vision, on the "big picture," you simply overlooked a lot of the details, which is another reason why you must strike a balance between your vision and the details. When you envision some aspect of your business and plan how much it will cost or how long it will take, identifying as many of the details as you can helps anticipate the true time and cost and allows you to make more accurate assumptions in your cash flow statement. I'm not saying that it is possible to think about every last detail, but ignoring too many details leads to wasting time and money.

A DUCK ACROSS WATER

To use another analogy, keeping your eye on the details is a lot like a duck swimming across a pond. On the surface the duck's forward movement appears peaceful and effortless. But, if you look below the surface, you'll see the duck paddling like crazy. Yet, even though the duck's legs are paddling like crazy, the duck never loses sight of where it's going. Building a successful business is just like the duck moving across the pond. You have to "paddle like crazy" to make it happen but you always have to keep your eyes on where you're going.

To help you get a better understanding of what types of details are involved in moving a business "across the pond," let's take another look at Ruth Owades and see how she put together the details that allowed her vision of Calyx & Corolla to become a reality. You might recall from Chapter 6, Ruth's idea was that her customers would use catalogs to order cut flowers and plants and have them delivered on the very next day. However, after Ruth came up with her idea, she still had to figure out all the details of how to make that vision happen.

As Ruth made the transition from step 1 (planning), to step 2 (preparation), she believed that the key to making Calyx & Corolla a reality would be her ability to develop the right strategic alliances. To help her do that, she identified and carefully followed the 28 tasks listed in Figure 8–1.[1] However, if you think about what's involved, you quickly realize that each of the 28 items had to be broken down into even more specific tasks. For

[1]Brokaw, 1993, pp. 96–104.

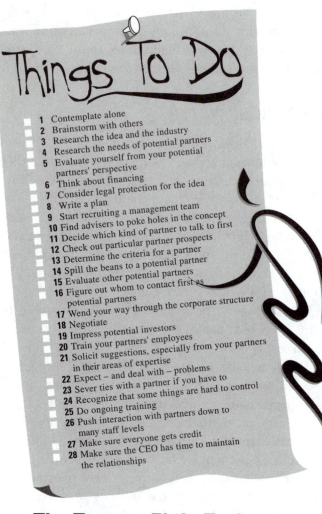

The Twenty-Eight Tasks
(Calyx & Corolla)
Figure 8–1

example, her third task, research the idea and the industry, was, as she said, a matter of sleuthing:[2]

> I went to the library and sat in front of the index and looked up everything—flowers, florists, marketing flowers, advertising flowers—to see what was happening in the industry generally, but also specifically with distribution.

And the same is true for each of the other 27 tasks in her list. For example, if you refer back to Chapter 7's discussion of how to put together a business plan, you get a feel for what's involved in Ruth's eighth item, writing a plan. As she described it:[3]

> The process of writing uncovered the logic of the business and brought up smaller questions—not megasubjects, like what are the risks—but what happens when the box is delivered and no one's home? Those little operational things needed answers from me.

In other words, her vision created the details and the details shaped her vision. You might think that Ruth's situation is the exception. After all, her vision required her fundamentally to change how the floral industry did business, and that's why she had to do so much. But that's wrong. It really doesn't matter whether you're doing something as drastic as changing an industry or something as "routine" as opening a retail clothing store in a mall. Every vision requires the visionary to identify and manage thousands of practical details. And all those details shape the vision. As an old saying goes, "The devil is in the details," because that's where all the work and the problems are but, paradoxically, that is also where most of the reward and the satisfaction are. There is simply no other way to build a successful business. For example, Tilman Fertitta, founder of Laundry's Seafood restaurant, a Houston-based 102-location restaurant

[2]Ibid., p. 98.
[3]Ibid., p. 99.

chain with revenues of approximately $190 million, "can spot a burned-out light bulb from his corporate jet."[4]

> Having spent his teenage years working in restaurants, Fertitta knows the business inside and out. We followed him on a tour of one of his establishments. "The lights aren't right," he says. "The music is too loud. We need an ashtray here."

Because the rhythm of business is ongoing, as you move your business forward, cycle by cycle, you need to keep paying attention to details. And when you're working on the details, like the duck paddling hard, you can't forget to keep looking up at your vision. You have to make sure that all of your decisions and actions fall within the context of your vision.

For example, when Ruth was deciding which strategic partner to talk to first—growers, shippers, or investors—all she had to do was look at her vision to know the answer was growers. If she wasn't able to locate one grower willing to do what she needed, there was no reason to talk to potential shippers or investors. According to Ruth, "It wasn't just finding someone willing to work with me. The growers had to meet certain criteria: quality, specialization in a particular flower variety, and commitment to service." As you can see, the criteria Ruth used in selecting which growers to work with were based on her vision. She answered the question of how she should decide with which specific growers to work by evaluating each of the available growers against her vision. By using her vision as the key criterion against which she could evaluate alternative actions, Ruth was able to move her business forward one paddle at a time.

Certainly, we can see what would have happened if Ruth hadn't identified a vision for her business or had a vision but didn't use it to guide her decisions. It's not that any given decision in and of itself would be wrong. Rather, she inevitably would have wound up making a series of **independent** decisions

[4]Christopher Palmeri, "Bill Clinton's Fish-House Friend," *Forbes* (November 18, 1996), pp. 126–129.

that, by themselves, were okay but cumulatively would not have led in the desired direction. That's because, in any given situation, there may be a difference between what's the best course to take in an isolated sense versus the best course of action to take in a contextual sense, relative to the objective of realizing her vision.

For example, if Ruth were deciding which growers to align herself with and was not using her vision, she very well may have chosen different growers. If she hadn't used her vision as the key criterion, she may have gone with those growers who offered her the lowest price or the most favorable payment terms, which would have given her a different business than what she wanted. However, because she evaluated them against her vision, she based her decision on items like quality and commitment to service. So, by focusing on her vision, she was able to make sure that all the details and all her decisions moved her business toward her goal.

SHARING YOUR VISION

Again, it's not just **your** decisions. The decisions of everybody involved must contribute to the realization of your vision, and it's your job to make sure that happens, whether you run the company or manage a department or project. If all of your employees understand, buy into, and internalize your vision then they, too, naturally will make the decisions that lead everyone along the same path, the path to your vision.

To get all of your employees' decisions focused on the company's vision, you will have to formalize many of the important details as the company grows. Remember Starbucks, Howard Schultz's business started in the early 1970s? Well, after 25 years, the company has grown to a 20,000-employee, $700 million a year corporate behemoth with a training program focused on the details. Allan Hickok, managing director of Piper Jaffray in Minneapolis, says, "They pay a lot of attention to detail, and everything the consumer touches drips with quality."[5]

[5]Jennifer Rees, "Starbucks," *Fortune* (December 9, 1996), pp. 190–200.

The company manages to imprint its obsession with customer service on 20,000 milk-steaming, shot-pulling employees. It turns tattooed kids into managers of $800,000-a-year cafés. It successfully replicates a perfectly creamy café latte in stores from Seattle to St. Paul.

. . . Starbucks is a company with a lot of rules, and all partners [employees] have to memorize them. Milk must be steamed to at least 150°F but never more than 170°F. Every espresso shot must be pulled within 23 seconds—or tossed. Getting it all down is one goal of the training program. . . .

TIM SHARES STREAMLINE'S VISION

Even before your company has thousands of employees, codified rules, and intensive training programs, it's important to maintain a group focus. Let's look for a moment at how Tim DeMello makes sure everyone at his startup understands and works toward his vision. At the beginning of Streamline's fourth customer interaction cycle (multiple products and services to 100 test customer households), Tim and his small but growing staff met to identify all of the detailed actions and decisions that needed to be addressed for this last test cycle. To facilitate the brainstorming process, Tim suggested that they divide the details into categories related to how the company was organized. In this way Tim could assign a specific individual responsibility for each action and decision identified in each of the six main categories:

- Customer resource center,
- Sales and marketing,
- Operations,
- Finance and administration,
- Information systems,
- Product and service offerings.

By the time the meeting ended some three hours later, the whiteboards in the conference room were covered with almost 500 individual items, as shown in Figure 8–2. As you can see from

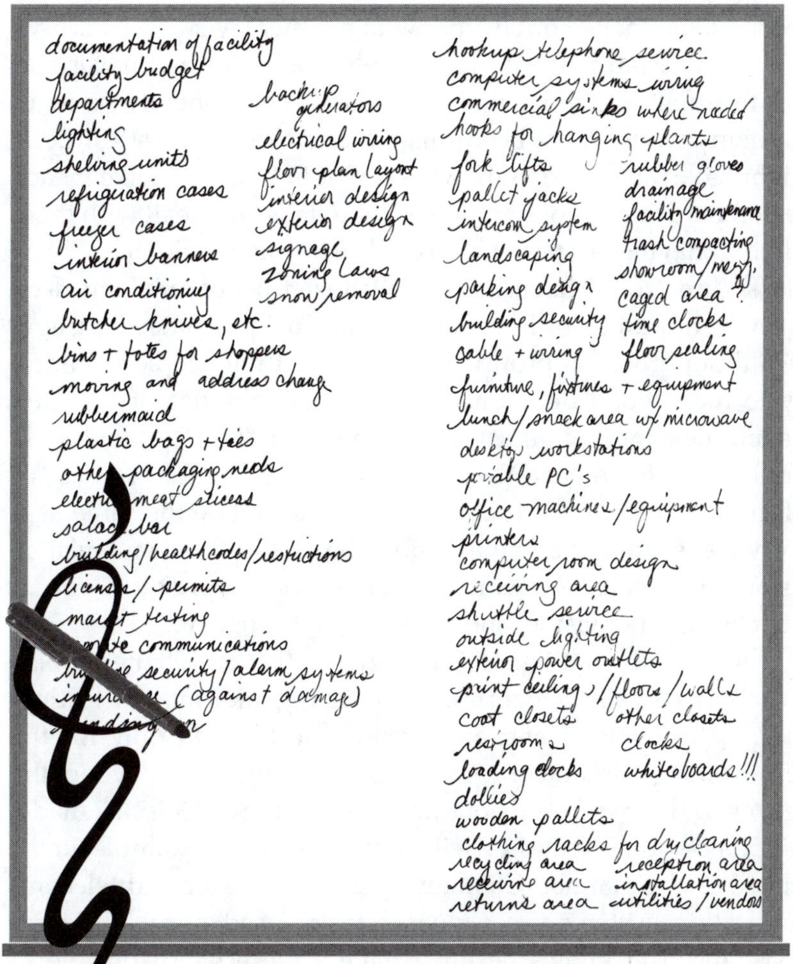

documentation of facility
facility budget
departments
lighting
shelving units
refrigeration cases
freezer cases
interior banners
air conditioning
butcher knives, etc.
bins + totes for shoppers
moving and address change
rubbermaid
plastic bags + ties
other packaging needs
electric meat slicers
salad bar
building/health codes/restrictions
licenses / permits
market testing
corporate communications
building security / alarm systems
insurance (against damage)

backup generators
electrical wiring
floor plan layout
interior design
exterior design
signage
zoning laws
snow removal

hookup telephone service
computer systems wiring
commercial sinks where needed
hooks for hanging plants
fork lifts
pallet jacks
intercom system
landscaping
parking design
building security
cable + wiring
furniture, fixtures + equipment
lunch / snack area w/ microwave
desktop workstations
portable PC's
office machines / equipment
printers
computer room design
receiving area
shuttle service
outside lighting
exterior power outlets
print ceilings / floors / walls
coat closets
restrooms
loading docks
dollies
wooden pallets
clothing racks for dry cleaning
recycling area
receiving area
returns area

rubber gloves
drainage
facility maintenance
trash compacting
showroom / merz.
caged area
time clocks
floor sealing

other closets
clocks
whiteboards !!!

reception area
installation area
utilities / vendors

Actions and Decisions
(Streamline, Inc.)
Figure 8–2

the list, some of these items are very specific, such as "get wooden pallets" and "get butcher knives"; whereas some, like "market testing" and "corporate communications" are more general and needed to be spelled out further with another layer of detail.

Think what it would have been like if Tim had never had that meeting and laid out all the details. Undoubtedly, some of the items would have been missed, and Streamline's test cycle might have failed. Or, think what it would have been like if each person made up his or her own list of details and dealt with them without having a shared vision. The result would have been chaos. Tim would have had a half dozen people making decisions on hundreds of important details, using whatever criteria each thought was appropriate. It's not that the people wouldn't try to make good decisions, rather, in the absence of a shared vision, their individual sense of "good" or "bad" undoubtedly would be different, and there is no way of telling the cumulative effect. But, there is no doubt that it would not be the same as if everyone shared the same vision. So, it's details and vision, vision and details. Remember, your company is not just you. It must be a shared vision, and it's **your** job to share it.

A careful reading of Streamline's list of 500 items also reveals two main categories. Some items, like market testing, specifically relate to and are intended to be used only for the next customer interaction cycle. Other items look beyond the next cycle. Once these actions are taken or these decisions made, the expectation is that they will stay in effect. For example, items related to the planned Customer Resource Center and telecommunication systems are expected to be used on a long-term basis, and Tim knows he must have a more hands-on role in these items.

As can be seen from Tim DeMello's, Ruth Owades's, and Howard Schultz's businesses, details make up a large part of the daily operation of a company and play a significant role in shaping the company's destiny. And you, as the CEO or manager, must see that everyone shares your vision and that every detail gets done. Regardless of how many customer interaction cycles you've completed or how big your business becomes, you must make sure that you always pay as much attention to the details as you did the day you opened. Just as you can never stop dancing with your customers, you can never forget the details.

DETAILS AID IN THE TIMING OF THE RHYTHM OF BUSINESS

Another extremely important role of details is in the timing of the rhythm of business, which if you remember means when you move between the steps in any one customer interaction cycle or when you move on to the next customer interaction cycle. In Chapter 5, we asked how Tim DeMello decided whether he was ready to begin a major expansion of his business or needed one more test cycle. Tim decided by noticing a blip in sales, and I want to point out that the blip was a detail, just one of the many details that Tim sees every business day. In this case, of course, it was a very important detail; and if Tim had not seen that detail (and in reality it could have been a very small change in sales), he would not have known that was the time to expand his business. Due to his close focus, motivated by his love for his business, he saw that detail and his intuition extrapolated a much larger conclusion, which was that he needed one more test cycle. Using one small detail to extrapolate to much larger conclusions is what intuition is. In Chapter 4, we said that, when we love someone, our intuition about that person grows. We notice a smile, a frown, or a pause that lasts a second too long and instantly our intuition is alerted. Why? Because of our love we've come to know that person so well that one small detail sends us a much larger message. In business we have to know our work just that well, because over and over again, these small details are the signals that something in our company is right or wrong.

The greater our intuition, the smaller the detail that will alert us and allow us to move faster and with greater confidence. For example, I remember, when working with Michael

Shane, we decided to try a 1-900 information provider business. We placed a few small ads in *The Wall Street Journal*. The first day that an ad ran, we had had about 30 responses by noon. But based on these responses, Michael decided to kill the other ads and completely change our tack. He immediately felt we were not going to draw the customers we needed. So, it is extremely important to pay attention to details, because they not only are what needs to be done but they are the signals that alert your intuition when to change or when to stand pat. And, the more quickly and the more accurately you can read such signals, the better your business will grow and the more likely you will satisfy your customers and beat out your competition. So, don't just try to get the details done, hear what they are telling you. Remember, in talking about successful businesses, Leo Kahn said, "And the entrepreneur has got to know when to change and when to be rigid in sticking to the original principle." And a key component of "knowing when to change and when to be rigid" is the details and what your intuition feels those details are telling you. Then, when you do change, you need to make sure everyone in your company understands and follows the new adjustment, so that your company grows in the direction of your newly refined vision. Oh, by the way, don't forget the ice cubes.

KEY POINTS IN CHAPTER 8

• Although it's important to get every detail done, it's also important not to become so overwhelmed by the details that you lose sight of your vision.

• Your vision creates reality and reality shapes your vision. And since reality is in the details, we also can say your vision creates the details (reality) **and** the details (reality) shape your vision.

• Identifying as many of the details as you can helps anticipate more accurately the true time and cost and allows you to make more precise assumptions in your cash flow statement.

• Because the rhythm of business is ongoing, as you move your business forward, cycle by cycle, you need to keep paying attention to details.

• You have to make sure that all of your decisions and actions fall within the context of your vision.

• The decisions of everybody involved must contribute to the realization of your vision; and it's your job to make sure that happens, whether you run the company or manage a department.

• Regardless of how many customer interaction cycles you've completed or how big your business gets, you must make sure that you always pay as much attention to the details as you did the day you opened. Just as you never can stop dancing with your customers, you never can forget the details.

• Another extremely important role of details is in the timing of the rhythm of business, which if you remember, means when you move between the steps in any one customer interaction cycle or when you move on to the next customer interaction cycle.

• When we love someone, our intuition about that person grows. We notice a smile, a frown, or a pause that lasts a second too long; and instantly our intuition is alerted. Why? Because of our love we've come to know that person so well that one small detail sends us a much larger message. In business, we have to know our work just that well, because over and over again, these small details are the signals that something in our company is right or wrong.

• The greater our intuition, the smaller the detail that will alert us and allow us to move faster and with greater confidence, saving time and money.

Even a mistake may turn out to be the one thing necessary to a worthwhile achievement.

…Henry Ford

9

Success and Failure

In Chapter 1, I said that you have to know how to plan for failure as well as success because both are part of the rhythm of business. But, before you can correctly plan for failure, you need to understand what it is.

We generally think of failure as not achieving a desired end in an allotted time. It's interesting that when we view failure this way, we believe that the "end" really is the final point, the stopping point, the last hurrah. And, further, we seem to believe that there is a predetermined time period during which we must reach that end. It's as if once we've gone beyond that arbitrary period the game is over and we have to pick up our marbles—if we have any left—and go home. Finally, we seem to feel an implied shame for having failed. We feel like characters in a Hawthorne novel, forced to wear the scarlet **F** for failure for all the world to see.

WHAT IS FAILURE?

However, successful businesspeople view failure very differently. They know that is not how the "game" is played. They know that whatever they're trying to achieve is never the endpoint. It's only one of many points they need to pass in the rhythm of building a successful business. And they don't worry about the shame of failure. To a natural-born businessperson it's not shameful, it's a lesson in what doesn't work. And, last, they don't worry about arbitrary limits of time. They keep trying until they succeed. But wait, you might say, time limits are not always arbitrary. Every business is constrained, if not by time, then by money, which isn't going to last forever; and those are certainly valid arguments. But, rather than prove the finality of a failure, those arguments are simply two very good reasons why it is even more important to plan for failure as well as success. With the proper planning, failure is simply an approach that doesn't work rather than the end of an entire business.

In Chapter 2, we talked about how Wang Laboratories had gone from a multibillion dollar success to a multibillion dollar failure. As An Wang unfortunately found out, the dance didn't stop once his company became a success. He stuck too long to an outmoded product, but if you follow the company's recent activities, you can see that the new CEO has brought the company back into profitability. He changed Wang from primarily a hardware company to primarily a software company and is building a successful business by satisfying a new set of customers with new products and services. However, these important changes have occurred only after billions of dollars in losses forced out An Wang (and his son) and a long stay in Chapter 11 bankruptcy allowed the company to recoup. Why? Because An Wang did not follow the rhythm of business, a rhythm that understands and plans for failure as well as success. In fact, the only reason Wang Laboratories was able to survive in the face of huge losses was because of the bankruptcy laws and because it had accumulated so much capital in the good days, when its hardware products were right.

PLANNING FOR FAILURE AS WELL AS SUCCESS

Remember what happened when Bill Gates first introduced Windows? Even though the expected sales of version 1 and version 2 did not materialize, Bill Gates knew he hadn't failed. Rather than saying, "That's it, we've failed," he studied the situation, listened to what his customers were telling him, made the necessary changes, and with version 3 changed microcomputer history. Bill Gates stuck with Windows through versions 1, 2, and 3, not through dumb luck, gritty determination, or because he could see the future (no matter how much it may seem sometimes, no one is prescient). It was part of Gates's intuitive understanding of the rhythm of business. Maybe Gates didn't know whether version 1 was going to be a success. Maybe he didn't know whether version 2 was going to be a success. Maybe he didn't even know whether version 3 was going to be a success. No one can know these things for sure. But Bill Gates could know and plan that he was going to market at least three (or four or five) versions of Windows over a four-year period. He could allocate the time, the people, and the financial resources for a product release that included failure as well as success. And that type of planning, following the rhythm of business, can make the difference between real success and real failure.

ANALYSIS AND REFINEMENT

It is true that Microsoft has many advantages in the software industry, but its greatest advantage is Bill Gates and his natural-born business skills. Again listen to Gates,[1]

> I think, throughout our history, we wake up every day knowing that in the business of technology—you have to think about, what are you missing? What is the research or customer feedback that you should be paying more attention to? And how do you keep that pace of innovation very, very high?

[1]Transcript from "The Road Ahead," *The Charlie Rose Show* (November 25, 1996).

Intuitively, Gates follows the rhythm of business and recognizes the extreme importance of the assessment and refinement period that follows each customer interaction. **And, the key part of assessment and refinement is recognizing both the successes and the failures**. After all, keeping the successes and changing the failures is what assessment and refinement is about. Whether the result of any customer interaction is primarily a success or failure, your company need never be permanently damaged as long as it retains the capability to assess, refine, and improve itself for the next customer interaction cycle.

Consider how Barry Diller, the former chairman of Paramount Pictures, Fox Inc., and QVC Inc., and now chairman and CEO of Silver King Communications, viewed failure as he set about building Fox, Inc.:[2]

> When outsiders predicted failure, I welcomed it. All they knew was that fourth networks had always failed before and even the Big Three were suffering a depressed market at the time. What they didn't know, what they *couldn't* know, was that we weren't interested in creating a *fourth* network. We were inventing an *alternative*.
> They based their conclusion on one set of expectations. Meanwhile we were free to operate on another. But we didn't find our voice immediately. **The truth is, our first shows were horrible. We were losing, just as everyone had expected. But we were also working it out, figuring out a process as we went along.** [Bold is my own]

For Barry Diller and Fox, producing each show was a new customer interaction cycle allowing the network to "work out" a better understanding of its customers and refine its programming to fulfill its customers' desires.

Sam Walton, the founder of Wal-Mart and Sams, was refreshingly candid about his numerous mistakes. In his book, *Made in America, My Story*, he said:[3]

[2]Diller, 1995, pp. 19–20.
[3]Sam Walton with John Huey, *Made in America, My Story* (New York: Doubleday, 1992), pp. 253–255.

I don't know how the folks around our executive office see me, and I know they get frustrated with the way I make everything go back and forth on so many issues that come up. But I see myself as being a little more inclined than most of them to take chances. Sometimes, of course, that leads me into mistakes. . . .

Our Hypermarts weren't disasters, but they were disappointments. They were marginally profitable stores, and they taught us what our next step should be in combining grocery and general merchandising.

HOW DEMELLO DEALS WITH FAILURE

Tim DeMello's experience at his first company, Wall Street Games, provides another good example of how successful businesspeople view and deal with failure. Tim's original idea was to create a game that imitated Wall Street's investment trading process, using play money. After much thought he developed and marketed what he billed as an "interactive board game," a package that contained everything the customer needed to "trade" shares on Tim's version of the stock exchange. Further, he planned that the customer would buy the package from retailers that sold traditional board games. The problem was that, after three months, only 100 units had sold; and Tim's new company was heading rapidly down the roller coaster toward failure. Rather than throwing in the towel, Tim analyzed all the information he had gathered from his customers and retailers and concluded that he needed to redesign the product and, more important, redesign how it was positioned. The changes Tim made were to sell the game direct to the customer as part of a three month investment challenge with prizes cosponsored through an alliance he developed with AT&T. During the five week period following the launch of his business with its new concept, over 10,000 units were sold. The customer had indeed voted, and what seemed like sure failure went on to become a success. As I mentioned earlier, Tim sold his interest in the company in 1992, for nearly $2 million.

Tim's experience with his board game, in fact, was instrumental in his developing an appreciation for the role problems play in building a successful business:[4]

> The most surprising thing, and one of the toughest I had to get through, was realizing I'm in the business of solving problems. And that problems are not a bad thing. When I started the company I was pretty guarded about the problems of the business. I would think, "Oh God, we don't have capital," or "Oh, jeez, we really screwed this up." And I would think I was really alone. Then I started thinking, how many of these problems are the result of growth? And 50% or 60% were. If you want to sit around and run a little shop, you won't have any problems. But if you try to grow, you have personnel problems, capital problems, servicing problems. I realized that even money is just another thing that needed to be solved.

FAILURE IS PART OF THE DANCE

As Bill Gates, Barry Diller, Sam Walton, Tim DeMello, and other successful businesspeople know, failure doesn't have to be failure if you understand what it really is and know how to deal with it. In fact, Gates is such a strong believer in the positive aspects of failure, he prefers to hire people who have failed in some way. He believes, "The way people deal with things that go wrong is an indicator of how they deal with change."[5] And as we've seen, change is an ever-present dimension in the rhythm of business.

An old Chinese saying translates to something like this: Every exit is an entrance to new horizons. Clearly, the person who expressed this sentiment must have been thinking about failure. Failure is not to be feared. It is not an end, it is simply a point along the path. Even more important, it is a message that something is wrong, and you need to find out what it is and

---

[4]Timothy DeMello, "Wall Street Games Inc.," in *Anatomy of a Start-Up* (Boston: Inc., 1991), p. 387.
[5]Patricia Sellers, "So You Fail. Now Bounce Back!" *Fortune* (May 1, 1995), pp. 49–66.

change it. Earlier I said that **success is never final. Well, the good news is, neither is failure. It is a positive part of the process. It is a part of the rhythm.**

Again, I want to emphasize that when I talk about failure I am not indulging merely in superficial, sentimental, psychological views of failure. I am not talking about those who see a glass as half empty or those who see a glass as half full. I am not giving a motivational pep talk, urging you to not let failure stop you. That's how it might look from the outside: That successful businesspeople are gutsy and determined and never let failure get them down. Sure that's true, but that is not the important point. The important point is that, on the inside, successful businesspeople know that, no matter how catastrophic a failure is, if you can learn from the failure and have sufficient reserves of time and money, the failure can be corrected. **Failure is not to be feared nor can it ever be totally avoided. Failure is a part of the natural rhythm of business.** So, the key issue is this: How do you plan for failure so that you learn from it and have sufficient reserves of time and money to turn the failure into a success?

FAILURE ITSELF IS A MATTER OF DEGREE

The main point in this understanding is to recognize that failure itself really is a matter of degree. The common concept of failure, as I mentioned at the beginning of this chapter, is of a problem so large that it cannot be solved in an allotted amount of time with an allotted amount of money. But every failure that fits that definition almost always begins as a small problem that grows large due to neglect or an incorrect interpretation of information. We know this because, if we saw a problem correctly in the first place, we would have solved it before it caused the failure. So, planning for failure is first a matter of learning how to deal with problems. If we understand how to deal with problems, we will understand how to deal with failure, because most failures are the result of small problems that grew so big they could not be solved within the allotted time and within the allotted money.

Now the question is, How do we deal with problems? If we look at the rhythm of business what we see is that "problems" are an integral part of every customer interaction cycle. Every customer interaction cycle consists of seeing a customer need, coming up with a flexible, low-cost business concept, testing it in the marketplace, analyzing the results of the test, and then refining the product and business concept according to what you learned from your analysis.

Failure therefore is any mistake that occurs during any part of a customer interaction cycle and during the analysis and refinement step (step 4), we locate the mistake and correct it. Failure is part of the process, because if every part of the customer interaction cycle were a success, there would be nothing to analyze. Our business would be a beautiful graph of one line heading straight into the stratosphere of infinite profits, the never-never land of the ideal business. But as we know that never-never occurs. Every customer interaction cycle has some successes and some failures. What we do is keep the successes and analyze the failures to see how we can turn them into successes. You might say, don't we also analyze the successes to see what we did right so that we can do it again? Yes, that's true. But, we do that only because the possibility of failure always lurks. If there were no chance of failure there would be no need to analyze success. **So, the essence of analysis is failure. Without failure, there would be no need to analyze anything.** The cure for failure and the way to deal with problems is by following the rhythm of business and paying particular attention to step 4, the analysis and refinement step. Through analysis and refinement, you see your successes, analyze your failures, and then make the necessary changes.

SKYMALL, INC.

SkyMall, Inc., recently was featured in *Forbes* magazine. SkyMall produces the catalogue shopping magazines stuffed in the seat pocket in front of you that you flip through between work, naps, and peanut snacks. I quote this article at length because it so clearly illustrates the importance of failure, and how disastrous it can be for a company **if it is not allowed to fail.** Paradoxically, if it is not allowed to fail, the company will not go through the analysis and refinement step and grow to become a success.

Here is almost the entire story as it was written in *Forbes*:[6]

> Robert Worsley, a determined red-haired father of six, got the idea for SkyMall on a flight from Seattle to Phoenix back in 1989. Paging through the Giftmaster catalog from the airline seat pocket, he was startled by its poor merchandise. "It had 6-foot pencils and fish ties," recalls Worsley, peering through preppy, tortoiseshell glasses.
>
> Worsley, now 40, had a brainstorm. With onboard telephones proliferating, it would be very easy for consumers to place their orders from airplanes. If only there were something worthwhile to order.

He's using himself as a customer to start the business.

> Why not create a catalog of catalogs, featuring pages from well-known catalogs like Land's End and the Sharper Image? Worsley figured a catalog with merchandise like that could blow out of the water the shoddy offerings made by Giftmaster, a tiny subsidiary of Minneapolis-based Carlson Cos., Inc.
>
> Phoenix-based SkyMall Inc. was born. . . . Worsley began by mailing 100-page business plans to 50 venture capitalists and individual investors. Writing the plan was easy for Worsley. He had spent five years as a Price Waterhouse accountant before quitting to become a financial consultant. He also kept his eyes open for investment opportunities.

He began by following the conventional wisdom, writing the business plan, and so forth.

> By February of 1990 Worsley bagged what seemed a dream investor—WordPerfect cofounder Alan Ashton. Over their first dinner

[6]Suzanne Oliver, "Spoiled Rotten," *Forbes* (July 15, 1996), pp. 70–73. Reprinted by permission of *Forbes* Magazine © Forbes Inc., 1996.

meeting, Ashton's wife wrote Worsley a $250,000 check. Worsley and two other investors chipped in $25,000 apiece, and SkyMall was in business.

Joy! Joy! He got his financing.

Worsley's original idea was to hand-deliver customers their orders as the travelers landed at airports. "If they can deliver a pizza in 30 minutes, why not merchandise?" he wondered. He thought that immediate delivery would appeal to busy executives who had forgotten to pack dress shirts or to buy anniversary gifts.

He **thinks** he knows what his customers want **but does he really**?

Executing the plan required building warehouses and stocking inventory near airports across the country. This was no small undertaking. But generous Alan Ashton was prepared to finance it. Whenever Worsley asked for more money, Ashton cracked open his checkbook.

He set up his business exactly as written in his business plan without compromises. He doesn't have to compromise. He has all that money from Alan Ashton.

With money so easily available, Worsley spared no expense. He bought a 21,000-square-foot warehouse and installed state-of-the-art technology at SkyMall's first location, in Phoenix. At his adjacent customer service center, he put in expensive Next personal computers linked by a Sun Microsystems server. All in all, he spent $3 million in Phoenix. "We fell in love with technology," Worsley admits, shaking his head at his own extravagance.

It's always tempting to spend too much on a business you love, but why not? Worsley has the money and he wants to do the best he can for those customers he thinks he knows.

SkyMall got off to a terrific start. By the spring of 1991 its catalogs were on board TWA and Continental. The airlines were happy to carry the catalog because Worsley paid them a percentage of sales and guaranteed to cover the fuel cost of carrying the catalogs if the commissions fell short.

He successfully negotiates alliances.

SkyMall's first catalog featured products from Hammacher Schlemmer and Spiegel. The catalog companies sold Worsley merchandise at a 35% discount so SkyMall could match the prices of the parent catalogs. Worsley stocked the merchandise at his Phoenix warehouse. If a customer landed in Phoenix, SkyMall hand-delivered the merchandise; otherwise it sent the package out overnight. Catalogers made a small profit, but more important, they got customer names to add to their mailing lists.

Worsley anticipated that one day he would confront Carlson Cos., the owner of Giftmaster. But he didn't expect that it would come so soon. In the spring of 1991 Worsley got a phone call from Walter Erickson, Carlson's senior vice president. He asked if Worsley wanted to buy Giftmaster. The Carlson catalog did about $6 million in annual sales and was just breaking even. After consulting with Ashton, Worsley decided to buy. The purchase cost Ashton several million dollars.

Is success about beating the competition or is it about pleasing the customer?

Worsley moved Giftmaster to Phoenix and slowly replaced its catalogs with SkyMall catalogs. Just a year after it started Sky-Mall owned the industry. It had catalogs on board United, Delta, USAir, Continental, TWA, and Alaska airlines.

But earnings didn't meet expectations. As it turned out, travelers burdened with luggage, briefcases and PCs weren't eager for more packages to schlep. SkyMall was bleeding $500,000 a month. Worsley couldn't take the stress.

Uh-oh—Guess what? He didn't know his customers as well as he thought he did.

One day in December of 1991 he walked into his kitchen, his neck swollen grotesquely. As his wife called 911, Worsley passed out on the floor. Another day, half his body turned hot, the other cold. At his company Christmas party, he developed horrible chest pain and was carried out on a stretcher. "I thought I was dying," he says.

He's on that emotional roller coaster ride heading straight down.

. . . Doctors diagnosed stress and told him to cut back, his big concession was to take weekends off. Over the next two years Sky-Mall opened airport facilities in Dallas, Denver, San Francisco, Los Angeles, Chicago and Atlanta. To unload excess inventory, the company opened two outlet stores. But the losses continued. In 1992 SkyMall lost $10 million, and in 1993 it lost $6 million. Alan Ashton and another investor continued to write Worsley checks, eventually sinking $25 million into SkyMall.

In a desperate attempt to create profits, Worsley created his own SkyMall catalog pages selling luggage, sports equipment, computer peripherals and pet paraphernalia. At one time, he had his own merchandise on 59 of the catalog's 130 pages. "On par it made sense to boost margins by buying merchandise at a 50% discount," says Worsley. Trouble was, Worsley couldn't sell the merchandise. And new software was misplacing orders and miscounting inventory.

He's attempting to analyze and refine his business now but is he listening to his customers or just trying to save his original vision?

At the end of the 1993 Christmas season, SkyMall had 20 trailers in its Phoenix parking lot, stuffed with extra suitcases, telephones, golf bags and watches. It owed 450 creditors $9 million and had just $500,000 in cash.

After discovering the extent of the software problem, CS First Boston canceled an initial public offering of SkyMall that it had been planning. A Baby Bell came close to buying SkyMall, but then backed out. Worsley pleaded with Ashton for another $6 million, but Ashton refused. Bankruptcy appeared imminent.

The roller coaster ride is heading down faster and faster.

... David Wirthlin, SkyMall's chief financial officer ... was answering 100 phone calls a day from SkyMall's creditors.

Expecting the Baby Bell purchase to come through, Worsley had offered his personal assets as a guarantee to SkyMall's printer. Now he faced losing everything. Worsley's eldest daughter asked his tearful wife, "Will my friends still like me if we're homeless?"

Stress from business affects **everyone** in the family.

Worsley holed himself up in his office for three days and developed a plan that saved the company. He realized that the whole concept was wrong. Yes, airline passengers had the time and inclination to browse catalogs. Yes, they were affluent customers. But, no, they didn't want the stuff so fast that they were willing to wait and pick it up at the airport.

At last, when near bankruptcy—when failure was hanging over him like the smell of death—Worsley decided to reassess his original vision. Desperation finally forced him to examine if his business needed major change, **not** just a jiggle to see if he could get his original vision to work. And, lo and behold, what Worsley saw was that he was not satisfying his customers. His company and his vision required a change.

No longer would SkyMall stock inventory or deliver at airports— 80% of SkyMall's customers received their merchandise at home anyway. Worsley had been trying to do too much. SkyMall had no business being in inventory and delivery. It should be in the business of prospecting for customers.

SkyMall would also begin charging catalog companies $20,500 per page to appear in the SkyMall Catalog. The investors liked the idea, but still wouldn't give Worsley money to repay his creditors.

So Worsley and his employees called SkyMall's creditors one by one to negotiate reduced payment schedules. Worsley closed SkyMall's airport locations. Hammacher Schlemmer, SkyMall's biggest catalog customer, helped out by buying $1 million of Sky-Mall's inventory. Worsley liquidated the rest.

At last SkyMall is profitable. The company earned a paltry $834,000 before interest expenses in 1995. But after a catalog redesign this year, SkyMall's weekly sales are up 44%. Worsley hopes to earn $2 million in net income on $53 million in revenues in 1996.

"In the end, I'm glad Alan didn't give us that $6 million," says Worsley, who has gained some perspective on SkyMall's travails. "It was like a parent teaching a child a tough lesson. We became more frugal and worked things out in a better way."

What led to Worsley's assessment and refinement? The key to his eventual success was failure. Ironically, for two years, the generosity of Alan Ashton kept him from failing. As long as money poured "from Alan Ashton's deep pockets," Worsley never was forced to see the basic mistake he was making. Worsley never was forced to truly analyze his business because he couldn't **fail**. The conventional wisdom is that most businesses fail from lack of capital, but here a business almost failed from too much capital. So, we can see that, again, conventional wisdom is wrong.

KEY POINTS IN PLANNING FOR FAILURE

I know, for some people, the idea of planning for failure is distasteful. It may seem somewhat like settling for second best or not trying for excellence. But, that is not really the case. Look at the human body. It certainly is one of nature's greatest creations, yet it is designed with failure in mind. If we cut our finger, our body heals itself. If we get a cold, our immune system fights off the disease. Our body is full of backup systems and defensive mechanisms. Look at evolution itself. It doesn't just include the possibility of mutation and change, it requires it! So, **planning for failure does not exclude striving for excellence**. Any excellent plan must include contingencies so that the plan eventually can succeed. Just as the human body plans for failure, so too must your business.

Here are some other key points to help you in the analysis and refinement of your business:

1. Keep a close eye on your customers and gather as much feedback from them as you can as to whether you are truly satisfying their individual wants and needs.
2. Give yourself clear and specific learning objectives for each interaction cycle and keep careful track of which objectives (milestones) are achieved, which are not, and why.
3. Prepare a cash flow statement for each interaction cycle, then compare your assumptions to the actual cash flow.
4. Provide a benchmark for your business by comparing it to the best in the field and, if you can, break down your business into its various components and analyze how each component compares to the best in the field, then find out what you can do to make that component the best.
5. Pay attention to details. By paying attention to details you can react to and solve problems when they are small. Small problems are hard to see but easy to solve. Big problems are easy to see but very hard to solve. Constant vigilance is essential and that means paying attention to details.
6. Failure is part of the rhythm of business. Remember that the essence of analysis and refinement is failure. No one can devise a perfect business right from the start. Every business and every project changes and grows and even the most successful business must change with its customers and the times.
7. Never lose sight of your vision and make sure every aspect of your business brings you closer to that vision. If the results of your analysis show that your business is not going in the direction of your vision, you must find out what is wrong and correct it. If your business is moving in the direction of your vision but not in the direction of profitability, you must find out if something is wrong with your business or if something is wrong with your vision.

The last point, finding out whether something is wrong with your business or with your vision is the most important, yet the hardest, kind of problem to solve because it goes to the very essence of your business. Again, think of An Wang. He had months and years of data telling him something was wrong and yet what did he do with that data? He must have pored over it again and again, trying to figure out what it was telling him but what he failed to realize (or if he realized, he refused to act on) was that the problem was not operational inefficiencies. His business was functioning as well or better than ever. But, his vision was wrong. An Wang needed a new vision of a new company that would satisfy the new needs of a new kind of customer; and this was really where he failed, in not changing or not realizing that he had to change his vision. It's easy to point a finger and think how An Wang was foolish, but his mistake is made repeatedly because changing your vision is very hard. The visions of who we are and what type of business we want are very intimate and important to us. I've emphasized that you must be in a business you love; so, if you do love your business, you must also love your vision of your business. It must be very important to you. Changing that vision is not easy. But, if you want to stay in business, you may have to; and if you can't, then it is time to get out (which An Wang and his son eventually did). That is the time to sell your business to someone who has the right vision for the new type of business your company needs to become to continue satisfying its customers.

Remember my own experience with the financial planning software. The product wasn't wrong nor the sales or advertising; our vision was wrong. We wanted to provide a product to a start-up entrepreneur who didn't want the product. When the company got the right vision—providing the product to the professionals who advise the entrepreneur—the product became successful. Over and over, I emphasize flexibility because it is such an important quality. And, your vision is the area where it is most important to be flexible. Yet, ironically, this is the one area where it is the hardest to be flexible. But you must, if your analysis tells you that your business isn't fitting customer wants and needs. And this type of analysis requires, as well as the ability to gather information and add up figures, a great deal of honesty.

BE RUTHLESSLY HONEST ABOUT WHAT IS RIGHT OR WRONG

Business often requires a certain amount of chutzpah, maintaining a front that your business is more established than, perhaps, it really is. In many ways that is part of business; but although sometimes you have to put on a front for investors, or customers, or employees, you can't kid yourself. You have to be ruthlessly honest about what is right and what is wrong. Don't deceive yourself into thinking a problem is something small; you can afford to ignore it, and it will probably go away. Don't think it's not worth the energy to solve because it's only a little problem and probably doesn't matter. Don't think that uneasy feeling in your gut is just some mushrooms you ate for lunch. When something is wrong, it's wrong, whether your head or your gut is telling you, and you have to fix it or see that it gets fixed. Furthermore, it has to be fixed now—today, not tomorrow—whether the problem lies in your business or your vision. Something wrong doesn't mean you're a bad businessperson, that you're a failure, or that you have no vision. It means that your first or second or third customer interaction cycle is providing you with the important information that your product or service or business concept or vision needs to change. Instead of being ashamed you should be proud that you have the insight and the honesty and the rhythm to see the necessity of that change, and if you have understood and followed the rhythm of business, you will have the flexibility and the financial and time reserves to make that change so your business can succeed.

FOUR-INCH, FOUR-FOOT RULE

One good, honest way to look at your business is explained in a rule I learned from a business associate I'll call John. John has what he calls the *four-inch, four-foot rule*. It happened this way.

John had made an investment in a new bicycle retail store. When considering the investment, he read the business plan, met with the entrepreneur, and looked at all of the standard things outside investors look at. He felt that the entrepreneur had done a great job of not only identifying his customers' needs but also had a really exciting business concept to satisfy those needs and differentiate his company in the marketplace.

Shortly after John made his investment and the store opened for business, his daughter needed to get a new bicycle seat and carrying rack. Naturally, John took his daughter to the store. The salesperson who waited on them didn't know John and didn't know that he had invested in the business. Not only was the level and quality of service disappointing, the store didn't have the seat or the rack they were looking for. They left very unhappy, and John very nervous about his investment. But John didn't leave completely empty-handed. He had his "**four-inch, four-foot rule**," which means you must always look at a business from two perspectives. First, you look at it from four feet. That is the view entrepreneurs and investors most often take—looking at the concept, the numbers, and the management team. Although obviously an important view, it is nonetheless focused on the big picture: the customers, how the business is going to satisfy those customers, and who is going to run the business. But, equally important, you must also look at the business from four inches, from the level of the details. You need to look at the business from the customers' perspective, up close and personal. You need to put yourself in the place of the customer to see what your business problems are and if your business in fact is satisfying them. Unless you take that up-close view, the perspective from four feet might lead you to the wrong conclusion.

I again look at our running example businessperson, Tim DeMello. You may recall that Streamline's second cycle of customer interaction was directed at only one customer, the DeMello household. Further, when the number of test customer households was increased to six during the third interaction cycle, the majority of the five new households were associated with Streamline. So, like Tim, you always have to look at your business through the CEO's chair (through the data) and up close and personal (from the perspective of a customer).

DEMELLO ANALYZES AND REFINES

Since we're talking about Tim, here's a real life example of how he used the analysis and refinement step (step 4) of the rhythm of business to discover, analyze, and solve a problem before it grew large enough to threaten his business.

As I mentioned, during cycle 1, Streamline provided dry cleaning services to 50 customers. After approximately seven weeks of interaction with his customers, Tim felt it was time to "pull back" and assess. Tim believed he had been in the market long enough to identify all of the positive and negative features of providing just one service to multiple customers and that he had enough data to figure out what changes he needed to make. As part of his information gathering, Tim asked his dry cleaning customers to complete the survey form shown in Figure 9–1.

As discussed in Chapter 6, a key observation Tim made during this cycle was the desirability of freeing the customer from being home when the dry cleaning van picked up or delivered. His customers wanted freedom from waiting for drivers, and his drivers wanted freedom from waiting for customers. The question was how to arrange that freedom.

While Tim was thinking this problem through, he went on a business trip. Arriving at his hotel too late in the evening for room service, he decided to eat some of the snacks and drinks the hotel provided in the in-room service bar. Following the instructions explained on a form, he checked off the items he ate, knowing that the cost would be added to his bill. The next day when he returned to his room he noticed that the hotel's maid service had replenished the service bar. At that instant, it "clicked" with Tim that the way to arrange the freedom both his customers and drivers wanted was to do what the hotel did. If

Dear Streamline Customer,

We could use your help. As a new company, it is imperative that we continually gather information from our customers. To this end, we've put together a brief survey and would appreciate if you would take a minute to complete it. The information we collect from the survey will provide us with a better understanding of how we can improve our service and fulfill your needs.

Simply complete the survey and return it in the enclosed envelope with your invoice payment.

Thank you in advance for your assistance.

Your friends at Streamline.

A. About You

1. Do you: own your home or rent?

2. Are you: married or single?

3. Are you: male or female?

4. What is your occupation? _____

5. What is your spouse's occupation? _____

6. Number of individuals living in your home (including children)? _____

7. Who in your home uses Streamline? _____

B. About Us

1. Was the welcome kit self-explanatory? Yes   No

2. Did you use the hook that was provided in your welcome kit? Yes   No

3. Do you use the order slips provided in your welcome kit? Yes   No

4. Are the order slips easy to use? Yes   No

5. How long did it take you to become accustomed to your pickup day procedures?
☐ Immediately ☐ 1 week ☐ 2 weeks ☐ 3 weeks   ☐ Other

6. Since you began using the service, what percentage of your dry cleaning has been done with
Streamline____%   Other____%

7. What additional services would you be interested in using?
☐ Shoe repair and polishing ☐ Storage of clothing ☐ Express service   ☐ Other_____

8. How satisfied are you with the quality of Streamline's service?
☐ Very satisfied ☐ Satisfied ☐ Somewhat satisfied ☐ Somewhat dissatisfied   ☐ Dissatisfied

9. What change(s) would you like made to Streamline's service?_____

_____

_____

_____

_____

Dry Cleaning Customer Survey
(Streamline, Inc.)
Figure 9–1

he placed a receptacle in the customer's home (i.e., an in-home service bar), he could deliver what the customer ordered and replenish it without the customer being home. Eureka!

After thinking through the service bar idea, Tim developed the design for a compact, efficient, and secure receptacle. I mentioned in Chapter 6 (see Figure 6–1) that it consisted of separate compartments for frozen, refrigerated, and dry goods; and that his drivers could install the receptacle easily in a home (or garage). Once the receptacle was installed, the homeowner would not have to be present to interact with the driver. Tim then worked with his father to actually build the service receptacle and install it in his garage, so he could test it during the second customer interaction cycle. In addition, he purchased a security key-pad for his garage door opener to allow the driver to gain entry to the garage to make deliveries.

From this one example we can see how Tim dealt with a small but critical problem immediately before it could rise to a level which could seriously damage his business:

1. He listened to his customers and to his employees and acted on what they said, both the good and the bad.
2. He didn't gloss over, ignore, or pretend a problem didn't matter. He knew every problem was critical and worked to solve it.
3. Because he loved his business, he thought about it all the time. Even when he was away on a business trip, on some level, he took the problem with him; so that, when a possible solution confronted him, he made the connection.
4. When he implemented the solution, he tried the idea on himself, "up close and personal," to see if it really worked.
5. Once satisfied the solution worked for him, he tried out a larger but still small-scale test, gathering information from his customers and drivers to see that the solution did indeed work, growing his business naturally, using "customer interaction cycles," and always analyzing and refining as part of every cycle.

In Chapter 2, I said that your overall objective is to use the best business concept to reach the point where you satisfy your customers' wants and needs as quickly and inexpensively as possible. In other words, the fewer the number of customer interaction cycles it takes to get close to the ideal business, the better off you are because each customer interaction cycle takes time and costs money. Consequently, if you reduce the number of cycles for your business or project to become profitable, you reduce the amount of money you need to implement the project and the possible equity in your business you have to sell to get it. The way to reduce the number of cycles is directly related to your ability to identify your problems, analyze them, and come up with solutions. In other words, problems and progress go hand in hand. Failure is not an end to the process. Failure is part of the process; the process is the rhythm of business; and if you understand the rhythm of business and plan for failure, it will play its proper role, which is merely as a step in the dance to success.

KEY POINTS IN CHAPTER 9

• You have to know how to plan for failure as well as success, because both are part of the rhythm of business.

• The important point is that, on the inside, successful businesspeople know that no matter how catastrophic a failure is, if you can learn from the failure **and** have sufficient reserves of time and money, the failure can be corrected. Failure is not to be feared nor can it ever be totally avoided. Failure is a part of the natural rhythm of business.

• Planning for failure is first a matter of learning how to deal with problems. If we understand how to deal with problems, we will understand how to deal with failure, because most failures result from small problems that grew so big they could not be solved within the allotted time and money.

• Problems are an integral part of every customer interaction cycle.

• Failure is any mistake that occurs during any part of a customer interaction cycle; and during the analysis and refinement step (step 4), we locate the mistake and correct it.

• The essence of analysis is failure. Without failure, there would be no need to analyze anything.

• Planning for failure does not exclude striving for excellence.

• Keep a close eye on your customers and gather as much feedback from them as you can to assess whether you truly are satisfying their individual wants and needs.

• Give yourself clear and specific learning objectives for each interaction cycle and keep careful track of which objectives (milestones) are achieved, which are not, and why.

• Prepare a cash flow statement for each interaction cycle and then compare your assumptions to the actual cash flow.

• Provide a benchmark for your business by comparing it to the best in the field; and if you can, break down your business into its various components and analyze how each component compares to the best in the field, then find out what you can do to make that component the best.

• Pay attention to details, so you can react to and solve problems when they are small. Small problems are hard to see but easy to solve. Big problems are easy to see but very hard to solve. Constant vigilance is essential and that means paying attention to details.

• Failure is part of the rhythm of business. Remember that the essence of assessment and refinement is failure. No one can devise a perfect business right from the start. Every business and every project changes and grows, and even the most successful business must change with its customers and the times.

• Never lose sight of your vision and make sure every aspect of your business brings you closer to that vision. If the results of your analysis show that your business is not going in the direction of your vision, you must find out what is wrong and correct it. If your business is moving in the direction of your vision but is not moving in the direction of profitability, you must find out whether something is wrong with your business or with your vision.

• The four-inch, four-foot rule means always looking at a business from two perspectives. First, you look at it from four feet, the view entrepreneurs and investors most often take— looking at the concept, the numbers, and the management team. You also **must** look at the business from four inches, the level of the details. You need to look at the business from the customers' perspective, up close and personal. You need to put yourself in the place of the customer to see what your business problems are and if your business in fact is satisfying your customers.

Part III

Let the Dance Begin

All glory comes from daring to begin.
...EUGENE F. WARE

10

Start Dancing

By now you should be very well-acquainted with the rhythm of business: attempting to develop a product or service that fulfills a group of customers' wants and needs, testing the product or service in the marketplace, analyzing the results of that test, and then refining the product or service to more accurately fulfill your customers' wants and needs. These are the four steps of what I call a *customer interaction cycle*, and it's very important to develop a feeling for the timing of when to move between each step. To do that, there are six requirements. You need, at least, some natural skill. You need to work hard and practice. You need a basic understanding of the mechanics of the business you are in. You need to gather information about your business (which includes paying attention to details, as we described in Chapter 8). You need constantly to think about your business. And you need to love your business with a passion. In this chapter, I want to discuss one additional requirement that brings everything together and makes your feeling and timing for the rhythm of business come alive. It is what I said in Chapter 4 that turns abstract love into passion. It is actually being in a business you love. **If you want to develop your feeling and timing for the rhythm for business, you have to be in business**. You can't wait to perfect your rhythm. The way to perfect your rhythm is by going to work every day in a business you love.

HOW DO YOU GET TO CARNEGIE HALL?

A story my father-in-law likes to tell illustrates what I mean. You might have heard the story before but it fits in so perfectly here that I'll repeat it. A woman visiting New York had tickets to a concert at Carnegie Hall. She didn't know how to get there so she stopped a distinguished looking gentleman strolling along Fifth Avenue, "Excuse me sir," she asked, "can you tell me how to get to Carnegie Hall?" The gentleman gave her a stern look and said, "**Practice! Madam, practice!**"

The gentleman is absolutely correct. To become successful in business, you have to practice, practice, practice. It's the second of the six requirements I listed for developing the rhythm of business, but when I talked about it in the first chapter you might not have understood what I meant. How do you practice business? Well, you can go to business school. You can read books about business. But, the most important way to practice business is by being in business! As I stated in Chapter 2, whether your business is large or small, old or new, corporate or entrepreneurial, the rhythm of business begins every morning when you open your doors for business.

A WALLFLOWER NEVER WINS

You can't win unless you're dancing. Yet, it's a point missed by millions, who timidly stay on the sidelines and never step on the dance floor, who never hear the beat. Ideally, by now you've gotten the point. **You will never learn to feel the rhythm of business unless you are in business**. Sure, business school is good. Sure, books are good. But, what brings it all together, what makes the abstract real, what begins the rhythm, what develops your love and passion, and what develops your feeling and timing for that rhythm is being in a business and making sure it is a business you love with a passion.

It doesn't matter whether the business is on a part-time or a full-time basis. It doesn't matter whether you start it by yourself, or with a partner, or work for someone else. It doesn't matter what your product or service is. It doesn't matter who your customers are. All that really matters is that you work in a business you love.

I've talked so much in this book about rhythms and feeling and timing, which are all abstract skills that can never really be taught, you may feel frustrated. But remember, while feeling, timing, and rhythm are skills that can't be taught, they are skills that can grow and they grow best when you are in a business you love. As I pointed out in the first chapter, you want to be in a business you love because that ensures that the other qualities you need will develop. If you love your business, you will work hard at it, you will develop the skills for it, you will understand the mechanics of the business, you will constantly gather information about the business, you will constantly think about your business, and then naturally and spontaneously based on the combination of all these ingredients, your feeling and timing will grow.

TIMING

Here's another story I like to tell when I discuss the importance of timing. One Sunday morning, my wife read in the paper that Isaac Stern, the world famous violinist, was performing at Symphony Hall that afternoon. Not surprisingly, when she called to get tickets she was told the performance had long since been sold out. My wife was disappointed, but tickets to an Isaac Stern concert sell out quickly. We resolved to be more vigilant and, when he next appeared in Boston, order tickets sufficiently in advance. We decided to head into Boston anyway and stopped for a drink at the Four Seasons Hotel at about 5 o'clock. An hour later, while we were waiting in the lobby for the parking attendant to get our car, a limousine pulled up and out popped Isaac Stern, violin in hand. As he walked into the lobby we stopped him and chatted briefly. Afterwards, I turned to my wife and said, "You see, timing is everything."

It's a humorous story but it does illustrate the point. Timing is very important. Unfortunately, neither feeling nor timing can be taught. As I said in Chapter 2, **feeling is your intuitive sense of something and timing is simply when you put your intuitive sense into action**. For instance, "feeling" is when Tim DeMello saw a blip in sales and felt his business was ready to go fully operational for its fifth cycle, or when Michael Shane saw a red flag in the number of calls, or when Greenberg noticed the potential for a hot product when his teenage girl customers bought just laces. "Timing" is when you act on your feelings, when you start the next cycle, when you start or stop an ad, when you license movie characters for your product. When your feelings are right, your timing has the best chance to be right. But since feeling is based on love and information, don't expect your timing ever to be perfect: Even if you love your business with a passion, you never will have all the information you need. You never will know your business or your customers or the economic environment perfectly. There always will be gaps, which is another reason why you need your feelings—to bridge those gaps. And if you are in a business you love with a passion, if you work hard at it, if you develop skills at it, if you understand the mechanics of it, if you constantly learn about it, and if you constantly pay attention to it, then when a small but significant detail pops out at you—that little blip in sales or that lack of response to an ad—you will be in the best position to bridge those gaps in your information and sense what the blip or lack of response is telling you. This intuitive sense grows naturally from love because, if you love something, you **want** to pay attention to it, you **want** to think about it, you **want** to learn about it and, just as your intuitive sense of your spouse grows, your intuitive sense of your business grows.

GATHER AND PROCESS INFORMATION QUICKLY SO YOU CAN MOVE QUICKLY

However, even if your intuitive sense of when to move between the steps of a customer interaction cycle is right, your company still has to have the capability to move at that time. If your company is slow, you may miss the time to move, even if you know it is the right time. If that happens, you may lose your primary selling season or your product may be out of date, or your customers' wants and needs may have changed. This problem is particularly important for larger businesses, as with the famous boondoggle of Ford and the Edsel. Ford's market research told the company in 1954 that the Edsel would sell, but the Edsel was not marketed until 1957.[1] As Ford found out from the Edsel's disastrous sales, you need to equip your business with the latest and best information technologies as well as the fastest design and production facilities, so that you can gather and process information quickly and then take advantage of that information.

However, as we don't live in an ideal world, the feelings and timing of the most intuitive businessperson may be off or the business may be unable to move as quickly as it should. That is reality. Mistakes happen. However, as discussed throughout this book, the rhythm of business is an ongoing process. Customer interaction cycles follow one after the other. So, if you follow the rhythm of business, you can correct the mistake and make adjustments in the next cycle. That is how successful business works. That's the process. That's the rhythm.

Larry Bird and Wayne Gretzky might have had great natural feeling and timing for basketball and hockey but, unless they played, those skills would never have developed. Likewise, Ginger Rogers and Fred Astaire or Stevie Wonder and Aretha Franklin might have had great natural feeling and timing for dance and song but unless they performed, those skills would never have developed. Similarly, Bill Gates, Michael Shane, Robert

[1]"Detroit Shoots the Works," *Fortune* (June 1959).

Greenberg, Ruth Owades, and Tim DeMello might have great natural feeling and timing for business but unless they began their companies, those skills would never have developed.

Of course, I'm not saying quit school and get into any business or start a business unprepared. I'm saying learn basic business skills, learn the fundamentals of your business, work hard. Know that you constantly have to gather, process, and connect information. Know that you always have to think about your business. And, most important, look to be in a business you love. That has to be your goal. Yes, sometimes you have to make compromises but life is too precious and the joys of being in a business you love are too great to compromise for long. And, if you want to start your own business, start it. Start small, start part-time, if you have to, but start it.

BEING IN BUSINESS UNLOCKS OPPORTUNITY

It's like planting a seed. Unless you plant the seed, the flower never will grow. Unless you start the music, the dance never will begin. Look at what happened to United Vision Group:[2]

> United Vision Group, in Ossining, N.Y., makes the kind of handsome wooden gifts you won't find at Wal-Mart. The company made its way to success by stepping rung by rung up the retail ladder. It's one of a very few *Inc.* 500 companies that have moved their products on pushcarts.
>
> Pushcarts? Don't laugh. With a good cart you can bring in $55,000 in a holiday season. "It's hectic when you open November 1 and close December 31," admits Joseph Coyne, a sales vice-president at United Vision. But the ruthless selling cycle taught the company invaluable lessons about product mix and product life cycles.
>
> From carts, United Vision stepped up to mall kiosks—temporary freestanding huts twice the size of carts. When several mall developers subsequently asked United Vision to take over vacant stores for a season, the company moved toward more sophisticated merchandising. The temporary stores' sales indicated sites

[2]Susan Greco, "Pushcarts to Success," *Inc.* (October 1995), p. 107.

ripe for expansion, and last October United Vision opened its first permanent store, called PG Arbor & Co., in New Jersey's Rockaway Town Square Mall.

Get the point! United Vision Group started as a pushcart business and grew to a store. But, if it had never started as a pushcart business, it would never have grown to become a store. **For growth to begin, there has to be a beginning. And, once there is a beginning, opportunity opens its door**. Once you've opened for business, if you follow the rhythm of business you may be surprised to see that the growth of your business occurs quite naturally, because the growth of business is an organic process. This is true for large and small businesses. As the business press is reporting on a daily basis, huge, global companies are constantly changing. AT&T is moving into the Internet and cable TV businesses. At General Electric, "Welch (the CEO) is pushing all of GE to take on a more entrepreneurial mind-set. This has clearly been his aim since he began reconfiguring the company 15 years ago."[3] Wells Fargo & Co. always is experimenting. Recently, it closed "22 traditional branches in the Sacramento area and opened dozens of less costly minibanks in such places as supermarkets."[4]

Your business will not always grow in the direction you intend. Rather, like some tree in a forest, it often will grow in completely unexpected directions. But this growth isn't wrong nor does it show a lack in your vision. One of the most important benefits of being in business is this quality of the unexpected. Almost unintentionally, you gather information that allows you to make connections about opportunities other than the one you currently are pursuing. We've seen this with every businessperson we've looked at, from Tim DeMello, to Robert Greenberg, to Richard Worsley. Businesses find profits the way plants find the sun—in the ways that nature provides, not the

[3]Tim Smart, "Jack Welch's Encore," *Business Week* (October 28, 1996), pp. 154–159.
[4]Linda Himelstein,"Wells Fargo Bets Big on Minibanks," *Business Week* (November 18, 1996), p. 160.

way the gardener necessarily plans. As Thomas Manning, founder of Buddy Systems, said in *Inc.*: [5]

> [C]ertain companies adapt well and certain companies don't. And the ones that adapt well make adjustments, whatever those adjustments need to be, whether they're investor composition adjustments, or adjustments in strategy, or adjustments in organization, or product changes. It can [range] from the very simple to the very complex, but that adaptation spells survival and possibly success, or at least the chance for success.

In the Introduction to this book, I mentioned McDonald's and H & R Block. Look at their stories.

> No sooner had Ray Kroc built national momentum for his Multimixer milk shake mixer than his company was nearly bankrupted. America entered a world war. An embargo on the domestic use of copper wiped out the supply of electric motors.
>
> Kroc scrambled to look for a product that would benefit from the war-time market. At the time sugar was so tightly rationed that it almost stopped the production of ice cream. Kroc became the national marketing agent for a new sugar substitute—corn syrup with a secret stabilizer.
>
> This experience taught Kroc a critical lesson: A company must react quickly to unforeseen changes in its market. When the war was over, electric motors and ice cream were available once more. He set out to revive his Multimixer business.
>
> Kroc wanted to find out why the McDonald brothers in California were buying so many Multimixers for their small drive-in restaurant. He had just gotten yet another order from them.
>
> When Kroc saw his first McDonald's he realized that it filled a huge void in the food service market. A McDonald's could be opened for as little as $75,000, including building and land, which made it perfect for franchising. It could be aimed squarely at the family market. And it sold more milk shakes than any other soda fountain he'd ever seen. Kroc decided to franchise McDonald's nationwide.[6]

[5]Thomas Manning, "Buddy Systems, Inc.," in *Anatomy of a Start-Up* (Boston: Inc., 1991), p. 404.
[6]John F. Love, *McDonald's: Behind the Arches*. New York: Bantam Books, 1986.

And at H & R Block:

> Henry and Richard Bloch started doing individual tax returns as a favor during the 1940s, but complained that it took too much time away from their "real" work, which was preparing financial statements for small businesses. The Blochs didn't realize that individual taxpayers desperately needed help: Tax forms were becoming increasingly complicated to understand and the Internal Revenue Service was beginning to phase out its practice of preparing them for free.
>
> The Blochs might have ignored the signs if it hadn't been for a customer who pleaded with them for assistance, convincing them to run an ad that offered to complete tax returns for "$5 and up." The result: a mob scene of eager customers. A year later, what had started as United Business Company became H & R Block.
>
> "The real danger comes from not adapting, from being afraid to make changes," observes Henry Bloch, who encourages his managers to act on new ideas . . .[7]

Thus, **the very act of being in business begins the rhythm that exposes you to information and ideas you never would have come across if you were not in business**. What's really exciting about this rhythm is that it never stops. The beat always continues. The dance never ends. As long as you are in business, new information, new ideas, new customers, new technologies appear. And like Robert Greenberg, Tim DeMello, Richard Worsley, Ruth Owades, Ray Kroc, and Henry and Richard Bloch, you never know where all that input will lead. But if you follow the rhythm of business, it will provide you with marketplace opportunities you never would have dreamed possible. It will allow you to make connections that change your business in ways you never would have imagined. Quite literally, it may change your life.

EVERYONE HAS RHYTHM

In Chapter 2, I said that, although you may be familiar with some of the steps in the rhythm of business, or even all of the

[7]Robert Ronstadt,"The Corridor Principle," *Success* (September 1988), p. 55.

steps, it is critical that you understand that they are not separate and unrelated but part of a whole, and the only way you understand this is by being in business. If you are going to build and run a successful business, you must learn what needs to be done, when it needs to be done, and why it needs to be done—and the only way you can do that is through the process of business itself.

The rhythm of business is not just another theory or philosophy. At its very essence, the rhythm of business is business. The rhythm of business is the process. Once you understand that rhythm, that process, you will never be able to look at business the same way again. Every business follows the same cycle of identifying a marketplace opportunity, getting an idea how to fulfill that opportunity, testing the idea in the marketplace, analyzing the results of the test, and then refining your business based on your new understanding and going back into the marketplace. That is how business works; and everything you read about, hear about, learn about, and practice about business falls somewhere in that cycle. Obviously, you need to understand millions of things that are not covered in this book: a million idea, a million techniques, a million angles. But, no matter what business you are in or how much time, cultures and technology change, one thing will not change, and that is the rhythm of business. **The rhythm of business simply is the way business is; it is how business functions**. And the beautiful thing about understanding the rhythm of business is that just understanding it allows you to follow the rhythm of business so much better and adds so much to your business skills. Just following the simple principles described here will change forever how you build and run your business and how you deal with everyday business events. The failures and successes no longer will be failures and successes but natural parts of a customer interaction cycle. The business concepts you develop will not be etched in stone but simply tests in an ongoing business evolution. The information you gather will not be mere data but keys to unfolding future market opportunities, and the love you feel for your business will not be something to hide or think of as mere pride but a major key to developing your own rhythm of business.

Essentially, you have two options. You can either learn to feel the rhythm of business and have that feeling shape your business life or you can ignore it or dismiss it. The choice is yours. Frankly, how you choose will greatly affect the success or failure of your business life.

I started this book with a saying from Zimbabwe:

> If you can walk
> You can dance
> If you can talk
> You can sing

That's the point. Everyone has rhythm. It's inborn to some degree in all of us. And, just as you can learn to feel the rhythm of dance and song, you can learn to feel the rhythm of business.

So go ahead. Work at your business. Love it. Grow it. Practice it. Feel its rhythm. It's the key to business success.

Let the dance begin!

Let The Dance Begin!

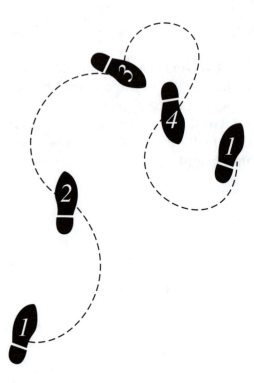

KEY POINTS IN CHAPTER 10

• If you want to develop your feeling and timing for the rhythm for business, you have to be in business. You can't wait to perfect your rhythm. The way to perfect your rhythm is by going to work every day in a business you love.

• To become successful in business, you have to practice, practice, practice.

• The most important way to practice business is by being in business!

• Your intuitive sense grows naturally from love because, when you love something, you want to pay attention to it, you want to think about it, you want to learn about it, and just as your intuitive sense of your spouse grows, your intuitive sense of your business grows.

• You need to equip your business with the latest and best information technologies as well as the fastest design and production facilities, so that you can gather and process information quickly and take advantage of the information that you find.

• For growth to begin, there has to be a beginning. Once there is a beginning, opportunity opens its door.

• One of the most important benefits of being in business is the quality of the unexpected. Almost unintentionally, you gather information that allows you to make connections about opportunities other than the one you currently are pursuing.

• The very act of being in business begins the rhythm that exposes you to information and ideas you never would have come across if you were not in business.

• If you are going to build and run a successful business, you must learn what needs to be done, when it needs to be done, and why it needs to be done, and the only way you can do that is through the process of business itself.

• Every business follows the same cycle of identifying a marketplace opportunity, getting an idea how to fulfill that opportunity, testing the idea in the marketplace, analyzing the results of the test, and then refining your business based on this new understanding and going back into the marketplace.

• The rhythm of business is not just another theory or philosophy. At its very essence, the rhythm of business is business. The rhythm of business is the process.

• Everyone has rhythm. It's inborn to some degree in all of us. And just as you can learn to feel the rhythm of dance and song, you can learn to feel the rhythm of business. It's the key to business success.

References

Bailey, Steve, and Steven Syre. "Retailer Leo Kahn Gets Back to Nature." *The Boston Globe* (August 21, 1996).

Bhide, Amar. "The Questions Every Entrepreneur Must Answer." *Harvard Business Review* (November–December 1996).

Bowers, Brent, and Udayian Gupta. "New Entrepreneurs Offer a Simple Lesson in Building a Fortune." *The Wall Street Journal* (October 19, 1994).

Brokaw, Leslie. "Twenty-Eight Steps to a Strategic Alliance." *Inc.* (April 1993).

Button, Graham. "The Superrich." *Forbes* (July 15, 1996).

Cortese, Amy. "The Software Revolution." *Business Week* (December 4, 1995).

Cringely, Robert X. "Notes From the Field." *InfoWorld* (January 15, 1990).

Davidow, W. H., and M. S. Malone. *The Virtual Corporation*. New York: HarperBusiness, 1992.

DeMello, Timothy. "Wall Street Games Inc." In *Anatomy of a Start-Up*. Boston: Inc., 1991.

Diller, Barry. "The Discomfort Zone." *Inc.* (November 1995).

Drucker, Peter F. *Innovation and Entrepreneurship: Practice and Principles*. New York: Harper and Row, 1985.

Fletcher, June. "New Developments: Same Frames, One-of-a-Kind Frills." *The Wall Street Journal*, September 8, 1995.

Gates, Bill. "The Road Ahead." *The Charlie Rose Show.* Public Broadcasting System, November 25, 1996.

Gerber, Michael E. *The E Myth.* Cambridge, Mass.: Ballinger, 1986.

Gleick, James. "Making Microsoft Safe for Capitalism." *The New York Times Magazine* (November 5, 1995).

Greco, Susan. "Pushcarts to Success." *Inc.* (October 1995).

Himelstein, Linda. "Wells Fargo Bets Big on Minibanks." *Business Week* (November 18, 1996).

Jacobson, Gianna. "Money Hunter Mindset." *Success* (November 1996).

Jefferson, David J. "Don't Walk a Mile in His Shoes." *Los Angeles Magazine* (December 1991).

Kahn, Joseph P. "Heartbreak Hill." *Inc.* (April 1988).

Kao, John. *Jamming: The Art and Discipline of Business Creativity.* New York: HarperCollins, 1996.

Karlgaard, Rich. "On the Road with Bill Gates." *Forbes ASAP* (Fall 1993).

Keough, Robert. "Shift in Focus Enhances Survival Odds." *The Boston Globe* (October 15, 1995).

Lavin, Dan. "Millionaires @ Work." *Fortune* (April 3, 1995).

Love, John F. *McDonald's: Behind the Arches.* New York: Bantam Books, 1986.

Manning, Thomas. "Buddy Systems, Inc." In *Anatomy of a Start-Up.* Boston: Inc., 1991.

Matzer, Marla. "Healthy Choice." *Forbes* (September 25, 1995).

McWilliams, Gary. "Small Fry Go Online," *Business Week* (November 20, 1995).

Oliver, Suzanne. "Spoiled Rotten." *Forbes* (July 15, 1996).

Palmeri, Christopher. "Bill Clinton's Fish-House Friend." *Forbes* (November 18, 1996).

Pine, B. Joseph, II. *Mass Customization: The New Frontier in Business Competition.* Boston: Harvard Business School Press, 1993.

Pine, B. Joseph, II, Don Peppers, and Martha Rogers. "Do You Want to Keep Your Customers Forever?" *Harvard Business Review* (March–April 1995).

Posner, Bruce G. "How to Finance Anything." *Inc.* (February 1993).

Redmond, Layne. "When the Drummers Were Women." *Earth Star* (August–September 1994).

Reese, Jennifer. "Starbucks." *Fortune* (December 9, 1996).

Reidy, Chris. "Cooking up a Recipe for Success Through Refining Product Mix." *The Boston Globe* (May 17, 1994).

Ronstadt, Robert. "The Corridor Principle." *Success* (September 1988).

Ronstadt, Robert, and Jeffrey Shuman. *Venture Feasibility Planning Guide: Your First Step Before Writing a Business Plan.* Natick, MA: Lord Publishing, 1988.

Sager, Ira. "How IBM Became a Growth Company Again." *Business Week* (December 9, 1996).

Saunders, Michael. "Brewing *up a* Storm." *The Boston Globe Magazine* (November 10, 1996).

Schmidt, Eric. "The Struggle for Bill Gates's Soul." *U.S. News & World Report* (November 25, 1996).

Sellers, Patricia. "So You Fail. Now Bounce Back!" *Fortune* (May 1, 1995).

Shane, Michael. *How to Think Like an Entrepreneur.* New York: Bret Publishing Limited Partnership, 1994.

Silverman, Stephen M. "Retail Retold." *Inc. Technology* (Summer 1995).

Slywotzky, Adrian J. *Value Migration.* Boston: Harvard Business School Press, 1996.

Smart, Tim. "Jack Welch's Encore." *Business Week* (October 28, 1996).

Smith, Raymond W. "Business as War Game: A Report from the Battlefront." *Fortune* (September 30, 1996).

Solomon, Stephen D. "The Best (Way)laid Plans." *Inc. 500* (1996).

Stevenson, Howard H., Michael J. Roberts, and H. Irving Grousbeck. *New Business Ventures and the Entrepreneur.* Boston: Irwin, 1994.

Taylor III, Alex. "The Man Who Put Honda Back on Track." *Fortune* (September 9, 1996).

Timmons, Jeffry A. *The Entrepreneurial Mind.* Andover, MA: Brick House Publishing Company, 1989.

"Tycoon." *NBC News*, May 26, 1995.

von Wersowetz, Richard O., Robert Kent, and Howard Stevenson. "Ruth M. Owades." Boston: Harvard Business School, 9-383-051, 1982, rev. 2/85.

Walton, Sam, with John Huey. *Made in America, My Story.* New York: Doubleday, 1992.

Welles, Edward O. "Virtual Realities." *Inc.* (August 1993).

Welles, Edward O. "Basic Instincts." *Inc.* (September 1996).

Wylie, David. "Calyx & Corolla." Harvard Business School, Case No. 9-592-035. rev. 1/9/95.

Index

A

Alliance partners. *See* Strategic alliance partners

Analysis and refinement step, of customer interaction cycle
    business example of, 199–202
    description of, 29
    failure and, 183–186
    function of, 188
    key points for, 195–196

Assumptions, for cash flow statement
    cash requirements, 132–136
    effect of assumptions, 128–129
    forecasting, 124, 126
    method for making, 123–126, *125*
    realistic presentation of anticipated needs, 136–139

B

Banks, money lending from, 142–144

Business
    competitive nature of, 24–25
    conventional wisdom regarding, 126–129
    core competence, 100
    effect of partnership on nature of, 156–157
    emotional highs and lows associated with, 59–62
    employees. *See* Employees
    failure and. *See* Failure
    feelings associated with, 15
    financing sources. *See* Financing
    goal of, 25, *26*
    honest appraisals of
        "four-inch, four-foot rule," 197–199
        importance of, 197

References in *italics* indicate figures

Butterworth-Heinemann Business Books . . . for Transforming Business

5th Generation Management: Co-creating Through Virtual Enterprising, Dynamic Teaming, and Knowledge Networking, Revised Edition,
Charles M. Savage, 0-7506-9701-6

After Atlantis: Working, Managing, and Leading in Turbulent Times,
Ned Hamson, 0-7506-9884-5

The Alchemy of Fear: How to Break the Corporate Trance and Create Your Company's Successful Future,
Kay Gilley, 0-7506-9909-4

Beyond Strategic Vision: Effective Corporate Action with Hoshin Planning,
Michael Cowley and Ellen Domb, 0-7506-9843-8

Beyond Time Management: Business with Purpose,
Robert A. Wright, 0-7506-9799-7

The Breakdown of Hierarchy: Communicating in the Evolving Workplace,
Eugene Marlow and Patricia O'Connor Wilson, 0-7056-9746-6

Business and the Feminine Principle: The Untapped Resource,
Carol R. Frenier, 0-7506-9829-2

Choosing the Future: The Power of Strategic Thinking,
Stuart Wells, 0-7506-9876-4

Cultivating Common Ground: Releasing the Power of Relationships at Work,
Daniel S. Hanson, 0-7506-9832-2

Flight of the Phoenix: Soaring to Success in the 21st Century,
John Whiteside and Sandra Egli, 0-7506-9798-9

Getting a Grip on Tomorrow: Your Guide to Survival and Success in the Changed World of Work,
  Mike Johnson, 0-7506-9758-X

Innovation Strategy for the Knowledge Economy: The Ken Awakening,
  Debra M. Amidon, 0-7506-9841-1

The Intelligence Advantage: Organizing for Complexity,
  Michael D. McMaster, 0-7506-9792-X

Intuitive Imagery: A Resource at Work,
  John B. Pehrson and Susan E. Mehrtens, 0-7506-9805-5

The Knowledge Evolution: Expanding Organizational Intelligence,
  Verna Allee, 0-7506-9842-X

Leadership in a Challenging World: A Sacred Journey,
  Barbara Shipka, 0-7506-9750-4

Leading Consciously: A Pilgrimage Toward Self Mastery,
  Debashis Chatterjee, 0-7506-9864-0

Leading from the Heart: Choosing Courage over Fear in the Workplace,
  Kay Gilley, 0-7506-9835-7

Learning to Read the Signs: Reclaiming Pragmatism in Business,
  F. Byron Nahser, 0-7506-9901-9

Leveraging People and Profit: The Hard Work of Soft Management,
  Bernard A. Nagle and Perry Pascarella, 0-7506-9961-2

Marketing Plans That Work: Targeting Growth and Profitability,
  Malcolm H.B. McDonald and Warren J. Keegan, 0-7506-9828-4

A Place to Shine: Emerging from the Shadows at Work,
  Daniel S. Hanson, 0-7506-9738-5

Power Partnering: A Strategy for Business Excellence in the 21st Century,
  Sean Gadman, 0-7506-9809-8

Putting Emotional Intelligence to Work: Successful Leadership Is More Than IQ,
  David Ryback, 0-7506-9956-6

Resources for the Knowledge-Based Economy Series

The Knowledge Economy,
Dale Neef, 0-7506-9936-1

Knowledge Management and Organizational Design,
Paul S. Myers, 0-7506-9749-0

Knowledge Management Tools,
Rudy L. Ruggles, III, 0-7506-9849-7

Knowledge in Organizations,
Laurence Prusak, 0-7506-9718-0

The Strategic Management of Intellectual Capital,
David A. Klein, 0-7506-9850-0

The Rhythm of Business: The Key to Building and Running Successful Companies,
Jeffrey C. Shuman, 0-7506-9991-4

Setting the PACE® in Product Development: A Guide to Product and Cycle-Time Excellence,
Michael E. McGrath, 0-7506-9789-X

Time to Take Control: The Impact of Change on Corporate Computer Systems,
Tony Johnson, 0-7506-9863-2

The Transformation of Management,
Mike Davidson, 0-7506-9814-4

What Is the Emperor Wearing? Truth-Telling in Business Relationships,
Laurie Weiss, 0-7506-9872-1

Who We Could Be at Work, Revised Edition,
Margaret A. Lulic, 0-7506-9739-3

Working From Your Core: Personal and Corporate Wisdom in a World of Change,
Sharon Seivert, 0-7506-9931-0

To purchase any Butterworth-Heinemann title, please visit your local bookstore or call 1-800-366-2665.